Blockade

01 02 03 04 05 29 28 27 26 25

Caitlin Press Inc.
3375 Ponderosa Way
Qualicum Beach, BC V9K 2J8
www.caitlinpress.com

Text design and cover design by Vici Johnstone
Cover image by Bernard Schroeder
Image on opposite page: Yaky Kop Cone, Quatsino Inlet, Vancouver Island. In the early 1990s, as an attempt to counter growing international criticism of logging practices in BC, the government brought in guidelines. Seen in this image is a "Scenic Fringe" as part of the government's "Visual Quality Objectives." Photo courtesy Garth Lenz.

Printed in Canada

Caitlin Press Inc. acknowledges financial support from the Government of Canada and the Canada Council for the Arts, and the Province of British Columbia through the British Columbia Arts Council and the Book Publisher's Tax Credit.

Canada Council for the Arts Conseil des Arts du Canada

British Columbia Arts Council
Funded by the Government of Canada | Canada

Blockade : diaries of a forest defender / Christine Lowther.
Lowther, Christine, 1967- author
Includes bibliographical references.
Canadiana 20250104466 | ISBN 9781773861609 (softcover)
LCSH: Lowther, Christine, 1967- | LCSH: Environmentalism—British Columbia—History. |
LCSH: Environmental degradation—British Columbia—Prevention—History. | LCSH: Direct action—
British Columbia—History. | LCSH: Civil disobedience—British Columbia—History. | LCSH:
Environmentalists—Canada—Biography.
LCC GE199.C3 L69 2025 | DDC 333.7209711—dc23

BLOCKADE

Diaries of a Forest Defender

by Christine Lowther

Caitlin Press 2025

Most of this book is concerned with events on Nuučaan̓uł (Nuu-chah-nulth) land, whose rainforests under threat are those of the Diitiidʔaatx̣ (Ditidaht), Pacheedaht, Qwabadiwa, ƛaʔuukwiiʔatḥ (Tlaoquiaht), hiškwiiʔatḥ (Hesquiaht), and ʔaahuusʔatḥ (Ahousaht) nations. This is the west coast of so-called Vancouver Island. I've lived gratefully in the Nuučaan̓uł territory of the Tlaoquiaht people since 1992.

In 1997, I self-published *A Cabin in Clayoquot* on spiral-bound recycled paper. It could have been called *The Blockade Diaries*, covering, as it did, direct actions to impede clearcutting of ancient temperate rainforests from 1991 through 1996 in both the Walbran valley and in Clayoquot Sound, where I still live. I've kept journals most of my life, recorded in the moment, as detailed as I could make them. They are the main source of this book. A thorough list of additional sources (Friends of Clayoquot Sound newsletters, recent online articles, books down the decades) is provided in the end pages. Although this is a memoir, it is more linear than some, perhaps a little on the 'zine vibe of narrative. A retelling from someone small who happened to volunteer in what turned out to be significant events. Others who were there may remember differently. As I worked nearly thirty years ago to prepare the manuscript, Joy Kogawa generously agreed to write its foreword, which is now my privilege to share again with her kind permission.

AUTHOR'S NOTE

There are many Indigenous place names in this book. While it is common to see traditional villages spelled with a silent "h"—for example, Hesquiaht, Opitsaht, Ahousaht—these words actually mean the people from these places. I recognize those nations' spelling of their homes: Hesquiat, Opitsat, Ahousat, while acknowledging that different authors spell these place names both ways. Additionally, I have tried to use "Walbran" and "Kaxi:ks" interchangeably. Same with Clayoquot Sound and Tlaoquiat.

Throughout, I have used a combination of people's actual names and, in some cases, anonymized names for privacy. Many individuals I knew or still know by their first and last name, and others only by a first name or a nickname. They are all real people whom I have met, worked with, or knew of, through the events and activities outlined in this book.

Vancouver Island from a float plane between Tofino and Vancouver, 2024. Clearcutting is still the norm and needs to be banned. Photo: Christine Lowther

CONTENTS

FOREWORD

by Joy Kogawa

"Trees are the sign of an active mercy in the world," says the narrator in *Itsuka*. "Year after year they continue to give us the breath of life." Having met young Chris Lowther, I am made bold to say that she too is a sign of Mercy's presence among us.

I first met Chris when she was a baby, sitting with her sister Beth in the living room of my friend, Pat Lowther. Most of us, especially in the writing community, know Pat's story. She was just about to step onto the larger stage of Canadian letters with a book of poems from Oxford. She was co-chair of the League of Canadian Poets. She was politically astute and deeply passionate about the world. I can still hear her soft, almost whispery voice as we walked and talked—mostly about our loves and our children and our despair. In those days my political awareness was below consciousness. I was in awe of her understanding.

I worried about Pat's little girls when she was killed but an intermediary who intercepted my letters suggested that my concern would not give them the normalcy they required at that desperate time. My letters stopped.

Imagine my joy, these many years later, to receive a phone call from Chris and to learn that she and her sister Beth were both well and thriving. I met Beth later and learned that the peacock feather I had sent them had been treasured all these years.

It may be fanciful, but sometimes I sense Pat's nodding face and her smile, and her finger pointing a direction. "We're connected, Joy, you and I, the trees, our kids, our lives and our deaths, yesterday and today and forever."

Amen, Pat.

And so here we are, reconnected not just in memory. At the end of a telephone, or sitting in a restaurant or in the living room, is a person who is by no means an apparition.

Chris's resemblance to her mother is uncanny, even to certain facial expressions. She also has the political energy and passion of her mother. To be invited to enter her intimate life, to share the truth of her personal experiences, to see the details of a young activist's day-by-day struggles and delights is no small privilege. How many of us watching the television news as it flits from story to story, know what it's like to actually be where the events are happening? Chris takes us into the forest, into the magic and the songs of resistance and the moment-by-moment journey of those who care enough to live their hope. Pat would be enormously proud. What parent would not be?

In a world of violence and environmental distress, here is a brave young writer pointing a direction of sanity. Come read and partake of health. It's a small miracle inside the big tragedy of environmental destruction. If we multiply such miracles, can we yet save the earth?

—Joy Kogawa, 1996

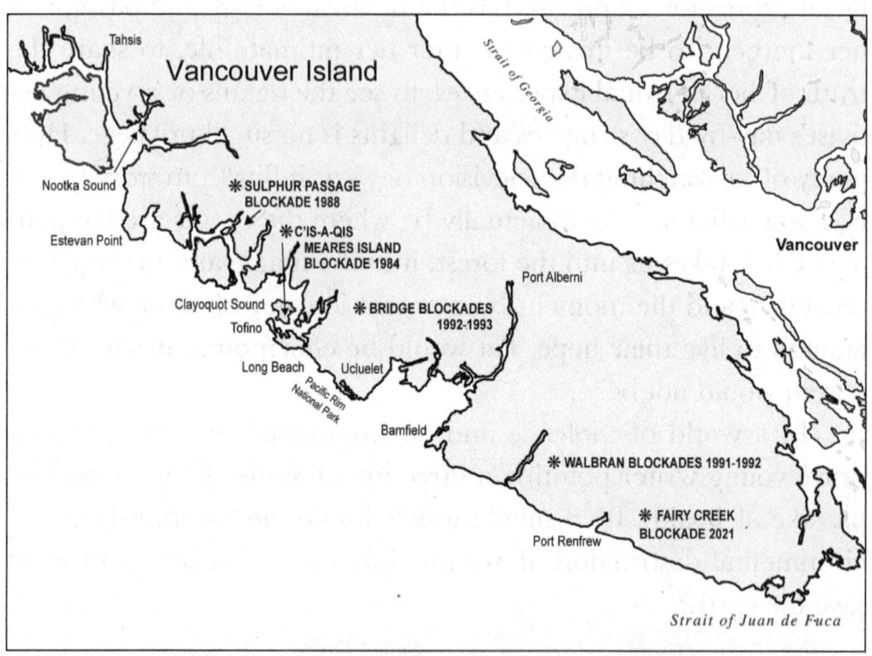

This map of lower Vancouver Island shows the approximate locations of the blockades and surrounding communities. The map is not intended for navigation.

INTRODUCTION

The province of British Columbia really needs a name change. George Vancouver was a British officer of the Royal Navy, and the mainland city named after him is on Sḵwx̱wú7mesh, Tsleil-Waututh, and Musqueam peoples' lands. I grew up there. Vancouver Island later became my home. It is a place of many peoples, and is three-quarters clear-cut logged. Here, visitors find a friendly and scenic land, often unaware of its histories of colonialism and civil disobedience. They might even believe the forests here are "saved." They come to surf, watch whales, kayak, camp, and hike on an island that's 456 kilometres long, containing cities and mountains, caves and complex ecosystems. Highways and malls, too. Indigenous histories of whale hunting, rich ocean abundance, and tending the forests—ancestral gardens; settler histories of fishing, mining, and logging, with tourism accelerating ahead of all.

In 1991, no one I knew had internet, a mobile cellular phone, or a digital camera. In the summer, two friends and I read posters on urban utility poles about blockades in the Walbran valley: Pacheedaht and Qwabadiwa territory adjacent to the Carmanah on the west coast of Vancouver Island. I had been signing petitions, writing letters and attending rallies for years, yet clearcutting was still the norm. Joining a blockade was the logical next step. We camped along the Walbran river, proper name Kaxi:ks. I hoped we could protect the entire west coast of the island against clear-cutting.

Temperate rainforests are extremely rare. In 1991 they covered about 2.5 percent of the area on Earth that was occupied by tropical rainforests. Occurring only in Chile, Norway, Australia, New Zealand, and on the northwest coast of North America, temperate rainforests occupy about 0.2 percent of Earth's land area. Who knew Canada held such global treasure? And why would anyone want to destroy such a scarce ecosystem? For profit, of course. Profit, made not by adding local value to logged trees by building Canadian homes with them, but by either raw log exports or pulping them to make toilet paper and telephone directories!

These are miraculous forests, full of young and old trees that sprout not from rich soil but from nurse logs that fall to the forest floor naturally. Mainly coniferous, these trees grow sometimes for two thousand years—if left in peace. This is rich habitat for everything from the mycelial network to large carnivorous predators. I am not qualified to elaborate on the science behind such wondrous life. But these forests are indeed what keep *us* alive.

In 1992, blockades happened to be farther north, at Clayoquot Arm Bridge in Clayoquot Sound. This system of valleys, elevations, and inlets held the largest tract of coastal rainforest left, and included the island's only cluster of intact, unlogged valleys. I didn't know about Mount Seghers in Hesquiaht territory, completely stripped of all forest cover and scarred with logging roads. And I didn't know about an area north of there, still in the Sound. The Escalante watershed looked like it had been napalmed, even from outer space. This was habitat erased for greed: the homes of black bears, cougars, wolves, bald eagles, osprey, marbled murrelets, and so many more. Spawning grounds of salmon were destroyed. Humans would also be impacted. Such vast "landscraping" contributed to the climate crisis we face now.

Clayoquot was to become a household name in Canada. For years, I pronounced it *Klack*-wot, but this is an anglicized version of ƛaʔuukwiiʔatḥ (Tla-o-qui-at), which isn't so hard to say, especially if you practise. I don't recall seeing him there, but a recent logger's memoir called the 1992 blockaders' camp "more like a love-in, a fun camping area to pass the time." On the contrary, it offered the structure of workshops and trainings to better prepare participants for various scenarios with cops, media, and angry loggers. Such classes had been available and honed since the '80s: A Council of All Beings, Conflict Management, Unlearning Racism, Nonviolent Civil Disobedience, Bioregionalism, Natural History of the Temperate Rainforest, and more. Even while many books don't mention the events of 1992, they often use that summer's photographs of police arresting people sitting on Clayoquot Arm Bridge. I was neither an organizer nor a leader, just one of many participants. The Friends of Clayoquot Sound (FOCS, also known simply as the Friends), ran these camps and blockades; several of their members had been in attendance at the Ministry of Forests' first old-growth strategy sessions.

Earlier blockades were history-making, high ground to build on. ʔaahuusʔatḥ Hereditary Chief Earl Maquinna George pledged to risk arrest, and was the first one apprehended on his own land at Sulphur Passage. His intention was to make a statement that the land was Ahousaht territory and it was both his right and responsibility to protect it from clear-cut logging. He was arrested by RCMP on the shoreline before even making it up the trail to the logging road. He had not been interfering with any machinery when arrested. For this reason, a judge dismissed the suit against Maquinna when he went to court.

In the late '80s, on the morning of the day they were to go to prison for blockading Sulphur Passage, a small group of women chanted "No more clearcuts" on the legislature lawn in Victoria, only to be begged by a prominent BC environmentalist: "Please stop—this is way too radical—you'll only be dismissed as extremists." She hastened to add, "They'll just think you're shouting 'No more haircuts!'" But billionaire multinational corporations were formidable foes. Decades later, not only does old growth still get logged, it is blockaders—and not forest pillagers—who still go to jail.

By the time the Peace Camp was established in 1993 at the "Black Hole," a razed and burned cutblock on the Pacific Rim Highway near the Tofino/Ucluelet junction, my partner and I had moved into a log cabin on an island near Tofino, and were learning how to paddle a pair of second-hand kayaks. We soon got to know harbour seals, river otters, great blue herons, kingfishers, minks, and even porpoises. The call of bald eagles was our morning alarm clock. Outside our door stood ancient, giant cedars. In such a spot, it was more than alarming when the cabin shook with road-building blasts from the not-so-distant Bulson valley.

The mass blockades of 1993 were highly effective. They showed everyone just how much the provincial government ignored the majority of its own people and was ruled by multinational clearcutting corporations. After the blockades, the province's New Democratic Party (NDP) government worked to appease the public by creating several new parks elsewhere in BC. Indeed, it seemed the government was happy to protect important areas as long as they were not Clayoquot Sound.

Indigenous Peoples here never signed treaties surrendering their lands to industrial extraction. Since I was arrested at Clayoquot Arm Bridge in July 1992, some pockets of Clayoquot Sound have been protected. But logging and salmon farming continue to damage ecosystems, while mining remains a threat. Some BC old growth ends up as pellets to be burned in Japan. Not long after things got real at Fairy Creek in 2021, a banner calling for protection of the Walbran was hung in Victoria, because such an effort remains necessary. The same month, the Sierra Club announced that a leaked BC Ministry of Forests old-growth map revealed that more than half of the province's most endangered ancient forests recommended for deferrals remain open to logging. And by logging, I mean largely clearcutting. Even after all this time, and all our work. Which just means we have to stay alert, informed, and active.

On June 18, 2024, the BC government announced it would, with the Ahousaht and Tlaoquiaht nations, protect 760 square kilometres in Clayoquot Sound by establishing ten new conservancies in areas that include old-growth forests. "In the process," Chris Hatch wrote, "the nations forced a local revamp of BC's heinous 'Tree Farm Licence' system—the 'TFLs' that reign across the province's 'crown lands,' effectively privatizing the living world into corporate satrapies." Statements from both Ahousaht and Tlaoquiaht said the conservancies would preserve ancient forests on Meares Island and the Kennedy Lake area, sites of blockades that led to hundreds of arrests.

"We will see Meares Island actively become real legislated protected areas for the first time in history," said Ahousaht hereditary representative Tyson Atleo. His people will invest in tourism, and look to generate and sell carbon credits as part of the benefits of the preserved forest areas, but will not sell to oil and gas companies. The agreement is supported by more than $40 million raised by the group Nature United, which said it will use the money to support two ʔaahuusʔatḥ and ƛaʔuukwiiʔatḥ nation conservancy management endowment funds, but also to compensate the forestry tenure holder.

"Pacific coastal rainforests, such as those in Clayoquot Sound, also hold vast amounts of carbon stored for hundreds of years, making them powerful natural climate solutions that will continue to sequester carbon while contributing to healthy air and water, ecosystem resilience and the well-being of communities."

—C.L.

THIRTY YEARS ON

In the summer of 2023, as the thirty-year anniversary of the 1993 logging blockades approached, I found myself rereading the late Jean McLaren's book *Spirits Rising: The Story of the Clayoquot Peace Camp, 1993*. Then, on August 9, the date three hundred arrests had occurred, a group text pinged at 9:30 p.m.

Valerie Langer sent: "Hey everyone, happy 30th anniversary of Mass Arrest Day! A turning point time. xox." Valerie had been on the board of the Friends of Clayoquot Sound, a leader, organizer, and spokesperson for blockades and other actions. She had been arrested numerous times.

Replies began to chime in.

"Wow! 30 years and yet we're all so young. Was this Midnight Oil day as well?"

"I remember your mom being so mad at your dad for spontaneously deciding to get arrested!"

"I slept over on Kennedy Lake that night and woke up to the sound of 1,000 people and Tzep [Tzeporah Berman] on the horn. I thought I was in a stadium."

"Loved that day … I was on comms so wasn't allowed to get arrested but will never forget 'If we all stand on the road, they can't arrest us all'—and then they did! Amazing day, amazing summer."

"A most memorable and meaningful summer."

"And don't forget those of us who got arrested the previous summer, before it was so cool to do so!"

"Still laughing at the 'Forest Tours' [arrestees'] bus 3 decades on."

"Hi all. I remember that day well. I was on probation but also had to shoot Midnight Oil for Greenpeace. Valerie and I slept at the bridge the night before and Share [BC] was checking vehicles leaving the protest. I was smuggled out under a bunch of luggage in the back of a Greenpeace van. Crazy wonderful times!"

"First you had to run through the bush to a pickup spot down the highway…"

"I remember how calm Tzep remained while being arrested off the side of the road."

"That was shock."

"Granny Jean [McLaren] and I were right at the front at the Midnight Oil concert because some drunken Share guys were holding a banner and trying to be disruptive. Jean and I were assigned to be the dancing peacekeepers, blocking their banner. Their energy really changed when the music started, suddenly they were rocking out and having a good time. They even offered us a swig from the Jack Daniels bottle they were passing around!"

A couple of days later, my phone pinged again.

"Just read that the Supreme Court has dropped the charges against 150-plus Fairy Creek protectors! On a technicality but even so!"

"Yesssssss!"

"Yup, in addition to some earlier ones. Only 400 to go. Blockades went back up a week ago. Hope to head down soon. Anyone want to go?"

PACHEEDAT, 1991

On the morning of Tuesday, July 23, my British friends Max and Pete blinked sleepily, pulled toques over their uncombed heads, and hoisted their backpacks. We made it to Duncan's Payless gas station by 6:15 a.m. Soon, a van full of people and luggage drove up and we piled in. Most of us were in our early to mid-twenties.

The NDP had just issued a cutting and road-building permit to New Zealand corporation Fletcher Challenge, ignoring its own old-growth strategy committee's call for a-two-year halt on logging in the Walbran. The company began cutting roads a week before the public input deadline expired. The public responded with local and international demonstrations, sit-ins, hunger strikes, tree-sitting, and roadblocks.

As soon as we hit the logging road, the contrast between the beauty of the forests and the gouged-out, desertified look of clear-cuts was shocking. Apart from stumps, only slash ("waste" wood) was left behind, along with the odd length of cable or other broken equipment. This carnage went all the way down to rivers and lake-sides, clogging the water with debris. After hours of endless moon-scapes, I was relieved and enchanted to see a doe and her fawn step out from some scrub.

How many miles did the clearcuts claim? Covered in dust, bumped and jolted and depressed, we finally reached our destination. As we stumbled out of the van, I started to laugh at poor Max. He looked like an old man: layers of dust like grey frost covered his eyebrows and beard.

Over our heads, a banner hung across the road: ONE FOR-EST, ONE FATE.

Placards lay everywhere, just waiting for eager hands:

BEAUTIFUL BRUTISH COLUMBIA

SUPER NATURAL B.S.

STANDING ON GUARD FOR WHAT'S LEFT OF CANADA

PACIFIC PLUNDERLAND

OH, CANADA

THE STUMPS ARE MY BONDAGE, THE FOREST IS MY FREEDOM!

LAND BUTCHERY AND WASTE

STOP MINING THE FORESTS

JUST SAY NO TO CLEARCUTS

THE MEEK SHALL INHERIT THE MOONSCAPES

Two young women were chained to a charred, uprooted stump pulled to the middle of the road. One was Dana. She was sixteen years old.

We had arrived in the heat of the moment, still cameras and video cameras clicking and whirring around us. A freelance news videographer was selling his coverage to the provincial CBC, while BCTV and CHEK had sent their own staff. Company vehicles lined the road. Fletcher Challenge employees began hauling logs out of their way. As the men finished, they stood over the two women. Dana lifted her head with confidence; her face wore a pleasant expression. Two police officers stood by. The rest of us waited on both sides of the road to see what would happen next. An impatient-looking man spoke.

"Are you willing to move aside and let us go to work today?"

"No, I'm sorry, I can't." Dana fought tears.

To the second woman: "Are you going to move?"

"I am not here to take your jobs away. But something in my heart tells me that we need to save this, for the young people, for your children—"

"For you," Dana piped in.

"What I want to know is, are you going to move aside and let us go to work today."

"I am not going to move."

A little girl of about six asked one of the loggers whether he would be "cutting any trees today." He answered curtly, "That's up to your mum and dad."

The man who had questioned the blockaders was a process server for Fletcher Challenge. He handed me some papers. I started to read them, but the legalese was baffling. Someone told me they proclaimed some sort of court order. I noticed several pages lying on the ground.

The company people left soon after the initial confrontation, with the police following like their hired escorts. One cop had said there would be no arrests for three days. I wondered if that would prove true, and why, and who decided. Why would he tell us such a thing? Was he sympathetic?

In any case, two young women had apparently stopped the clearing of an ancient forest. Minutes after the media had gone, when we were all cheering, a few loggers reappeared and sat down, watching us. Someone with a scarf wrapped around his face came down from a tree singing lyrics by Starhawk:

> We are the power in everyone,
> we are the dance of the moon and sun,
> we are the hope that will not hide,
> we are the turning of the tide.

Gradually, the loggers went one way and the rest of us went another: to the main camp. I didn't know that I'd soon be singing that song too, and often. I didn't dream that, over time, I'd come to hate the sound of it.

The next day I didn't get up with the others at six to join the blockade, a few minutes' drive away. I struggled with guilt, but cherished the lie-in and journal writing time.

This campsite was different from the upper Carmanah, where I'd been tenting in March. For one thing, it wasn't in the middle of a gigantic clearcut. The road here ended with a bridge over the

Walbran/Kaxi:ks river, and between it and the forest was a communal kitchen full of donated food. Dinner would come together around the fire under the tarp.

A path went into the forest beyond. All trails were fairly new at the time; one went halfway down to the ocean, not yet finished. No one got paid for trail building. It was all volunteer labour, organized by the Carmanah Forestry Society.

Fletcher Challenge's plan was to extend the road past the bridge, obliterating kitchen, trails, and forest. But a placard declared: THE ROAD STOPS HERE.

The riverbank was the best place to be. It was a village of tents in all the colours of the rainbow. Between setting up our (blue) tent and cooking veggie burgers down on the rocks, we were receiving a fast education. This was not some conveniently distant place; this was my home province, and its forests were the front lines. I couldn't believe I'd never realized the extent of the attack until now. In over thirteen years of schooling in North Vancouver, why had I never

July 23, 1991: our first ever blockade, Walbran valley / Kaxi:ks. Dana is seated in the middle of the road. Max stands between placards. Photo: Peter Cressey

been informed that BC, Canada, contained much of the world's original temperate rainforest, which took ten thousand years to evolve? Valerie Langer would later write, "Canadians found out that they had a rainforest in their country at the same time as they found out that it was being destroyed at an alarming rate."

Thanks to fellow activists, we learned that these forests develop in areas of a moderate maritime climate typified by at least 1,000 millimetres of rainfall spread out over at least 100 days and by a minimum of frost and snow. They generally occur less than 150 kilometres from the coast. Their tree species are those that are able to regenerate in shade below dense canopies like western hemlock, western red cedar, Sitka spruce, Douglas fir, and shore pine on the outer coastline. There was a lot I didn't know. When did we learn that these were the ancestral gardens of Indigenous Peoples? The same peoples who were forced onto reservations and into residential school?

I'd certainly introduced Max and Pete to my country's problems, yet this was a reflection of the whole planet's condition. A couple of days ago, we'd been hanging out on a grass verge near the Nanaimo bus depot, feeling like vagabonds, our stomachs full of veggie hot dogs. We blamed Max for attracting imbibers asking us where we were going; they always headed for him first. He was a small, bearded man with messy hair and well-worn clothes. His soft voice and educated English accent usually surprised them. We'd caught a bus to Duncan, the pickup point, and spent the night in a dusty patch of woods next to the highway. We were too tired to pitch the tent. And now, in the Walbran valley, hungry insects filled the humid air.

We spent all day at the upper falls. On our way there, I mentally prepared myself for the nudity of the bathers we'd see, saying nothing to my two friends. I wanted to be confident and casual ("chill" was not yet a hip term). I doubted the two modest Englishmen would strip off, and I wasn't about to myself.

Upon arriving, I studied the water under the falls and saw that it was perfectly clean, unlike the river at the blockade site, which was choked with debris. Let's call the waterfall Kaxi:ks Falls. Given the insulting name of "Fletcher" Falls by the logging company, it poured down over a wall of stone into a spacious pool where we swam. The pool was divided into two halves by a ridge of rock. We stood on this ridge for a shower from the falls. Below the pool were rapids, climbing rocks, "Jacuzzis" and small, round, still basins clear through to the bottom. Below all this was the largest pool, almost a small lake.

The water was a clear jade green. Tadpoles slipped through it; newts crept along the bottom, returning my stare with their tiny black eyes. Dippers, those birds that dance along the shore and walk underwater on the river floor, made several appearances. My two friends and I climbed up past the top of the falls where we found deep moss-green pools, one after the other, divided by narrow rapids or falls and dangerously strong currents. Max and I went as far as the spot where the river suddenly turned still, shallow, and lake-like. Pete left us to continue farther. He often went off on his own. I wanted to do some of that, too.

Looming protectively over our tent were two massive cedars. At night the miracle of their existence was somehow closer to being within reach; in the darkness they seemed awake, watchful, and wise. We never forgot why we were there. After spending my mid-teens organizing petitions and letters against cruise missile testing, followed by my early twenties in England demonstrating in the freezing cold against mink farms and live exports, chasing fox hunts across the muddy countryside with a bottle of garlic spray, yet still seeing injustice everywhere, blockading felt hopeful. Even as a last resort.

But a few mornings after we joined the effort, Fletcher Challenge and the police walked into camp and arrested young people who continued to sing their hearts out even as they threw themselves in front of approaching company trucks. A man from immigration was looking for foreigners, so in solidarity I ran into the forest with Max, Pete, and another English guy named John, whom Pete had met on the airplane. Later, he was nicknamed

Wild Man John. He was covered with sores where horseflies had bitten him.

We were like hunted animals, squatting on a mossed bank of the still green river. Beautiful mists rolled silently in among the trees. A kingfisher dived, caught a tiny fish, and ate it in front of us. And all of this was to be destroyed.

We decided to keep going and ended up on a long, wet hike up to Maxine's Tree, the largest known Sitka spruce in Canada. We trekked past dozens of giants along the way. What made Maxine's unique was that its huge, living diameter continued all the way up. I couldn't see the top.

After dinner that night back at camp, a meeting took me by surprise. It began with a "go-around," and I balked at public speaking. This was a large circle of impressive activists. But when I said Max and Pete had been dragged into this all the way from Britain (as if they had no wills of their own), folks laughed in a friendly way. I saw that people appreciated activists coming from so far to help.

Soon I realized we were planning not just a blockade, but our next move in the defence of the west coast. Discussion was open; nobody was coerced into any actions. Everyone got up from around the fire to build obstructions at 11:00 p.m. I was cold, wet and tired, with various aches and pains, but as soon as I was in the swing of good, hard work all my discomforts disappeared. By car headlights, we made perhaps four barricades of rocks and logs. It was empowering, especially when I worked with two other women alone. With a winch on a pickup, a huge tree trunk that the loggers had left behind was pulled across the road for the finale.

Next, everyone moved up to the first blockade site, the one we had faced when we first arrived. Another barricade was quickly erected there, with the addition of three large logs and boulders that were winched out onto the road. It was half past two when we finally found our beds. I slept like one of our barricade logs.

❦

Wake up call was tardy—about seven. This time Max and Pete lay in while I got up and into the back of a vehicle with nine children who had turned up late the previous night. Their family had a tradition of travelling together to places of conflict. They were religious, but trying to convert others was not their style. They had spent five months living on the West Bank, and a month in Jerusalem. All nine kids looked at me with the same eyes and the same relaxed confidence.

In front of the main barricade, a car blocked the road, with a woman I'll call Freda lying under it, her neck U-locked to the chassis. U-locks were possibly the most popular and versatile lock-down devices known to activists and law enforcement agencies alike. They were cheap, with no assembly required, quick to deploy, and relatively easy to conceal. The better ones needed more than bolt cutters to dispatch.

I was given the car keys, as well as a hand held radio. The latter didn't work, but I pretended I was giving information to others in the forest. The process server looked at me uncomfortably, so perhaps he bought it.

Freda's two support people were arrested immediately. This was a nasty surprise. The cop was angry. He shouted: "I said you are under arrest! Get over to the truck, NOW!"

A quick defining note on support people here. An arrestee's support person is present in close proximity to the arrestee, to witness and support in an emotional way, to boost morale, and to keep their activist informed regarding what is happening around them. When the cops close in, this person must move to the side of the road, out of the "contempt of court" space. Cops are meant to ignore support persons, not arrest them. Support people are also responsible for physical objects like the arrestee's vehicle and any medications. They track whether the arrestee has been held or released from police custody in good condition.

When arrested themselves, they can carry out none of this work.

It took ages for police to cut Freda out of her lock with a blowtorch; she sang legendary folk musician Roy Bailey's "Song of the Exile" through it all in her strong, deep voice.

Finally, she was carried away and a road grader easily dislodged all our hard work. The workers had grim determination on their faces, sometimes—it seemed to me—tinged with regret. There was an angry one who drove close beside us, knocking off our side mirror.

At times, when the loggers were at work in the forest, one of our bunch would run around amongst the trees, calling out. This person was called a runner. It was a small attempt to slow down the cutting by causing confusion. The cops brought in dogs to deal with runners, so it was a dangerous job. There was sporadic tree-sitting too; when Freda was singing as they blowtorched her lock, another strong voice had joined her from high up a tree. Tree-sitting can postpone logging longer than ground-based blockades. Cops would need to bring cherry pickers, a fire truck, or quickly erected scaffolding all the way to the action, unless they are trained and equipped tree climbers themselves. But there was talk of another logging company moving in: MacMillan Bloedel. We had been told that Mac Blo were known to start cutting trees with activists still in them. "We could do sustainable logging," that company had said regarding a particular tree farm licence in 1990. "But then we'd have to do it everywhere."

The worst thing about the planned road extension was that it would give access not only to the Walbran, but to other valleys—including the Carmanah, Logan, Sandstone, and Cullite—which constituted much of the last remaining intact rainforest areas on the island. This multivalley ecosystem made strong, viable habitat for many vulnerable species. There could have been countless unknown or not-yet-discovered creatures depending on these forests.

We were all being filmed and photographed extensively. One policeman strolled, by himself, with his video camera rolling, right into the main camp. An activist donned a mask as another said,

"It's nice to know we're living in a free country." Still another asked, "How do you feel about this personally?" The officer answered, "Look, don't get me wrong, I think these trees are beautiful. I have a job to do and I'm just carrying out my job. Don't get me wrong."

As that day's first trees fell there was deafening, growling thunder that rolled across the sky. We needed more blockaders.

I learned that the forest constantly changed as we hiked through it: so many different turfs and terrains, so many giants growing out of glass pools overhung with moss. At the trail junction to Beach Camp and Pacific Ocean path, we decided to venture off-trail and follow a stream bed down to the river. Some of the rocks formed amazing shapes and textures, smooth looking yet gritty to the touch, bright white with plenty of "handles." When we reached the river itself I gaped at the otherworldly sight of beautiful marble-like canyon walls, maybe four and a half metres high, framing the swirling creek. Each wall was cream and brown and white; little caves had been carved out by centuries of moving water. Pete and I scaled the walls as far as we could. The clear green water must have been delicious to swim in on a warm day. We walked along the bank for as long as possible before turning back. Bright pink flowers shone beside tiny exquisite-smelling purple ones. I didn't know their names, of course. What were they, blooming in late July? In the midst of utter serenity, we came upon two more marble-like walls on the far side of the water; one of them seemed to be an entirely different type. White and curved, it cast a reflection on the water that reminded me of Salvador Dalí images. The name Marble Canyon stuck. I looked around and asked Pete where Max had got to. "He's down in the water. He's starkers."

Since then, I've learned about karst ecosystems. These landscapes are created by water dissolving soluble bedrock, such as limestone. This erosion forms underground openings, caves, and passages for streams. Karstscape provides the drainage and nutrient recycling that results in impressively large old-growth trees. Logging such areas creates conditions for desertification.

I recall writing in my journal on the shore of Anderson Lake, far up the trail in the opposite direction, past Maxine's Tree. Max and Pete had gone exploring. I was experiencing tranquility with a hovering depression. The logging company wanted to turn the trail into a road. The lake lay in the very centre of a snug valley cradled by forest-fur-coated mountains, a true "wilderness," as I would have called it then, without roads. It was a landlocked lake, and for thousands of years the surroundings had protected it from white "civilization." The threat of clear-cut logging seeped into the peace I found there. I had trouble grasping that such a place could be endangered by greed, and was reminded of the threat by little jabs to my consciousness: the sudden alarm call of a bird, or a fish jumping, making soft ripples on the water. The knowledge felt like a disease in the air immediately around me; I was a carrier.

There was a unique kind of trout that lived only in the lake. Maybe that's what kept surfacing, causing a bubble or two and a ring of ripples. Imagine: it still lives nowhere else in the world! I also watched damselflies, dragonflies and salamanders. Anderson Lake, I whispered, I have a terrible secret. I cannot tell you; I cannot warn you. There is nothing you could do to save yourself. We will try.

My clothes were spread over the rocks in the sun, after a day's long downpour. Even my sleeping bag was wet. I hadn't yet heard of such things as thermorests or foamies. Sleeping damp and rough all night, the three of us crammed into such a puny tent, I had dearly hoped for sunshine to arrive in the morning. Now, under blue sky and fluffy white clouds, even my coat and boots were drying. It had been nice to lie awake listening to the rain, imagining all sorts of sounds. I was sure an animal prowled around us. John said he'd seen a bear twice since arriving in the valley.

Pete and I had attended the previous day's action while Max helped prepare food for tree-sitters and runners, one of whom was arrested later in the day. We were becoming negative, thinking that every day Fletcher got in and did some logging was our defeat. On the contrary, our presence each morning was a victory. They would never be unwatched again!

One day there were no blockades. Instead, a group of us waited to talk to the employees. We situated ourselves at the end of one of their roads, before the cutblock. I'd never seen a freshly felled area before and was shocked. It looked like someone had gone through with a giant machete. In a few months it would look like any other clearcut: the bodies removed, piles of debris covering the ground, the sawdust gone, a sea of stumps staring at the sky. The land would be ravaged and forgotten.

Fletcher Challenge had no fewer than eight cops with them, and all tried to pass us, but Bobby Arbess insisted, "This is very important information." He was the son of Sol, who had driven us in from Duncan. Held precariously in Bobby's hand was a large clump of thick moss, its dreadlock-like pieces hanging down. He held it up for all to see. As the CHEK 6 news cameraman zoomed in on it, Bobby said he'd got it from the cutblock, and that this moss was the preferred nesting habitat of marbled murrelets, rare seabirds that nest only in old-growth trees. It had taken a hundred years for scientists to figure out that these birds would leave the sea at dawn and dusk and fly to the forest to feed their single chick. Even the local Indigenous nation (the Tlingit, in Sitka) had said that none of their people had seen a nest. Bobby went on: it was apparently "illegal to log in any area which might be home to the bird. Fletcher Challenge has *said* they are doing research on these birds."

Another activist then asked to be read the injunction. That's the court order I'd had such a hard time understanding. To get an injunction against people physically impeding logging operations in this part of the Walbran valley, the company had applied to the BC Supreme Court. And it was still tedious to listen to, all that legal lingo. When the reader finished, the activist exclaimed, "I still don't understand it!" There was a pause. "Those are our lungs in that forest. And if you think that's a crock, go in there and take a deep breath." Suddenly Barney, a beagle, trotted into the cutblock, climbed up onto a stump and proceeded to defecate.

"Right on, Barney!"

"That's what Barney thinks of clearcuts!"

Laughter. Then we watched the fallers go in to work. I supposed we were lucky Bobby was not arrested.

The eight cops made us move away from the falling zone. After a while we heard a tree fall to the ground. To me, the only thing that compares with that horrific sound is road blasting. Several people howled loudly, cupping their mouths to send their mournful cries in the direction of the fallen tree. I wondered if the faller heard them.

We camped for the weekend on the riverbank, off the trail near Maxine's Tree. I was conscious of every noise I made in that quiet place. Even the scratch of my pen drafting poetry: something about dirt-filled fingernails, loam on my forehead, reforming as a salamander slipping through cold water. Shape-shifting between canyon walls. Asleep under the stars stirred only by an owl's hoot or a trout's ripple. Something unsophisticated about ferns and moss. *Hold onto the Great Grandmother Globe / Hang onto her intergalactic earlobe / Swing precariously like five billion dangly earrings / Cling to the one hospitable ball of blue in the universe.*

I ended up having to retreat into my tent to escape the ruthless mosquitoes reproducing in clouds over the water and in the forest. A living haze of insects danced chaotically like tiny drunk fairies, for hours. As I lay in my sleeping bag, the high-pitched hum of these tiny rulers-of-the-bush drowned out the sound of the creek. They were always waiting just outside the flap. I now admit that even they are beautiful. They have a kind of grace in their total surrender to movement.

On Sunday, the lads decided to take a challenging hike to Auger Lake. I hoisted my pack and hiked back to base camp on my own. At last, alone in the forest! I went slowly, nibbling juicy red huckleberries, and was startled by a rufous hummingbird who hovered near, checking me out. Our riverside tent site was vacant of other blockaders (probably because we left some damp clothes hanging there). I scrounged a snack from the kitchen and went swimming at the falls. It was cold and exhilarating. Someone filled me in on what we missed that past Friday: a tree-sitter came down from his perch and was mobbed by two cops in camouflage gear.

Rumour said that our camp might be illegal on the coming Monday. I wasn't sure what that meant. Maybe the company was trying to get "no camping" added to the court order. We were worried and gloomy, having been so glad to be there, making a difference, meeting wonderful humans, learning so much. I believed that if my mother had been alive, she would have joined in. Before her life was cut short at the age of forty, she was an activist and a poet. Some of her poems were about trees, forests, mountain ranges, waterways, and sea creatures. The League of Canadian Poets named an annual prize after her, the Pat Lowther Memorial Award. When my sister and I were little, Mum took us picketing around two ancient trees threatened by a development near where we lived in south Vancouver. The trees were cut down, but evidently Mum planted the seed of tree defence inside us that day.

At the largest fire circle so far, everyone gave their name, where they came from, why they'd come, and how they felt about the situation. All ages were represented, including two elderly women who'd been demonstrating and campaigning for decades, the now-late Melda Buchanan and Ruth Masters from Friends of Strathcona Park. Melda said she had been fighting for the environment for decades and won almost none of those battles. She grieved that extraction corporations are never charged with any crime, yet young people are taken away for defending nature. Ruth was responsible for nearly all the clever placards and banners, both what they said and the actual painting of them. She also gave out serving spoons, which she dubbed Hero Spoons. Engraved with "Walbran Blockade 1991," she called them "trophies, but practical." She even played "O Canada" on the harmonica during arrests. It emphasized the irony of "kids being hauled off to jail for defending the natural beauty of Canada … glorious and free."

We made our plans and all went to bed in high spirits. This base felt friendlier than my 1987 visit to Greenham Common Women's Peace Camp in England, but I had been on my own then, and younger, where bailiffs had evicted us daily, and we'd been trying to block convoys of nuclear weapons. Activists had thrown buckets of paint at the cavalcades. It is said that those actions and the women's permanent presence were what forced Prime Minister Margaret Thatcher to abandon her plan to keep US President Ronald Reagan's nuclear missiles on British soil. Direct action gets the goods.

Monday morning a "Ma Mu" group was up listening for marbled murrelets at 4:30 a.m. Others were in high tree platforms at 5:30 a.m., looking for murrelets and their nests. Most of us went to the blockade about an hour later, joining those who always slept there. A few stayed behind at base camp, as usual. Under our banner that spanned the road, BEAUTIFUL BR*U*TISH COLUMBIA, logs and boulders had been strewn, and a fire made. We were talking about doing some sort of spiritual ceremony as an effective blockade, since people have legal rights to practise their religion anywhere, perhaps even in the middle of a logging road. But we decided against it. A chanting woman made a heart shape out of stones on the road.

Our drummer sounded a slow, steady beat. The loggers pulled up, for once without media or police escort. The driver in the first truck got out and went back to his colleagues to talk. Meanwhile, a woman quickly and quietly slipped under his truck. When the driver returned, she was U-locked to his axle. "Jesus Kuh-rist," he said upon seeing her there. We cheered. The logger locked his truck, hopped in someone else's, and the Fletcher convoy departed back the way they came. We were singing as they left.

We waited for hours, in the hot sun and cold shade. Clearcuts have extreme climates. Finally, a helicopter descended, stirred up a cloud of dust, and went away again. In a few minutes it returned and let the truck driver out; he came toward us smiling, took something out of his truck, relocked it, and went back to the chopper. Its departing noise and dust seemed intentionally directed at us.

After a while, the food ran low and people trickled back to base camp. Sometimes we sang:

> If we have courage we could be healers;
> like the sun we shall arise.
> We are alive as the trees are alive.
> We have the power
> to fight for their freedom.
>
> —Rose May Dance and Starhawk,
> "We Are Alive"

How liberating just to rise every morning, wash, and not worry about my appearance. The conversations and connections I had with others were infinitely more important, more meaningful. When a fellow camper did some face painting on us, it was the first time I had looked in a mirror for six days. As for my two friends, their skin had grown brown and rough like bark. They would walk out of the forest with burrs and twigs stuck to their clothing like new growth.

The three of us had run out of film. I was running low on diary pages. I wanted to record every detail: tents, kitchen, placards, people, art, children, dogs. A week felt like a month. Away from the city, time passed slowly. It was the most healing sensation I had ever experienced, and I knew we were lucky. If only everyone could try living at a slower pace at least once in her or his lifetime. It might be the essence of true health. It would take me a while longer to learn that my bliss was not necessarily everyone's.

I looked forward to some things (chocolate), but dreaded leaving. I hated goodbyes. One brief journal entry reads: "A platform sways high up on a bare, candelabra-topped dead tree—a cedar 'snag'—right next to the main path. Jodi says this tree is the guardian. She hears it speak to her: 'If I go, we'll all go.' Not if we can help it!"

One morning, Max and I slept past seven, missing the rides up. We later learned that police easily picked a lock that held someone to a vehicle blocking the road, and our barricades were soon bulldozed. Three people were arrested holding a spiritual circle.

Two cops ventured down to base camp to inquire about an arrestee's young daughter. I asked them what their feelings were regarding the rainforests, the clearcutting, and the criminalization of forest protectors. One said: "We're not given a chance to think about it." The other declared, "If I were off duty, I'd be up here fishing and hiking. As agents for the courts, we're caught in the middle."

In the falling zone, a logger cut the branches under a tree-sitter's platform and made threats as the sitter clung in terror to his tree. When he asked the logger how he felt about being responsible for a death, the logger answered that he'd "bury him." Other loggers—and cops—were *laughing*. Our next idea was to sue the police for negligence. They had not once behaved neutrally, nor had they appeared—as they claimed—to be "caught in the middle." They appeared to be working for Fletcher Challenge. Of course, they had to carry out the court order, removing individuals who disobeyed it. But I'd often see cops and company supervisors talking quietly together away from the crowd, with their eyes on one or another individual forest protector. Or a cop would be nodding in agreement and saying "okay" to the process server, who was hired by the company (for the longest time I had assumed he was part of the court).

We had two occupied trees at camp (just in case) and four in the felling zone. I helped paint a big banner for one of them: LOVE 'EM OR LEAVE 'EM. Hot work, after which I slipped away for a refreshing swim at one of the most beautiful spots of the river, the sparkles on its surface folding and refolding in the breeze. Cold. Framed by thickly forested hills and cliffs, no other soul around.

Max planned to get his film developed into slides so that he and Pete could do a Walbran slide show for Friends of the Earth groups in Canterbury and London. I would buy a set from them and find an FOE group in Shropshire, where my college course was due to begin in September. There was apparently already a boycott on Canadian paper products in England. I wondered how many people over there knew about Canada's rainforests. The three of us were determined to add to that number, whatever it was.

Five of us stood on the road the next morning. We did pretty well, considering there was a large convoy to meet us: various different corporation vehicles, a grader, a company ambulance, and two RCMP paddy wagons with dogs in the back. A grumpy faller told me that unless a certain pickup truck was moved out of his way, it might meet a similar fate to another activist's van (a slashed tire).

I felt the need to keep covering my face with my scarf because of the cop with the video camera. He made it clear that he was annoyed with me for doing so, remarking, "This is beginning to look like Oka." The Oka standoff had been barely a year ago, across the country. Media images from that resistance had shown Kanyen'kehà:ka (Mohawk) warriors with their faces covered.

The cop even shot video of my book, Thoreau's *Civil Disobedience*. He was later caught snooping at someone's pack. Was that legal? What was he looking for? I caught him copying from an address book! He and an independent videographer who'd been camping at the bridge had showdowns, standing mere metres apart, "shooting" each other. On top of it all, this cop had been poking his video camera into people's tents early in the mornings, a rude and startling awakening. A violation.

We followed the convoy down to the falling zone, stopping to make some noise for the benefit of our tree-sitters in there. As a hummingbird zoomed in on me, suddenly a part of the convoy split off, and we got word that it had gone to base camp. We arrived, breathless and anxious, at camp. Two policemen were hanging around being watched by wary activists after one of the former had filmed some tree-climbing equipment. That was all. No surprise arrests or eviction.

Later, I sat journaling on the shady, mossy bank of the deep emerald-green pool. It was time to go and find some dinner. Pete, Max, and I were preparing to depart. We had tickets for the Stein Valley festival, although we all felt torn about leaving.

There was a group of five Toronto women with whom I would stay in touch. Bee, Corrinne, Maggie, Lynette, Kathy. All in their early twenties, they were already advanced gardeners, wildcrafters, herbalists, and artists.

From the blockade site, the forest that looked down on the valley loomed like an impenetrable wall of green, a flat mirage of one-dimensional trees with a spiky top. It reminded me of an enormous stage prop or a giant natural dam, trying in vain to hold back the sky as it poured over the edge, a bright blue screen spattered with rushing altocumulus. The sky was baffling at any time, anywhere in the forest. The longer I stayed, and the closer I looked, the more astonishing the natural world became. The breezes were cleansing, the air soothing and mild. Alas, the green wall was not impenetrable. The prop was removable. And removing it was "profitable."

On Thursday, August 1, 1991, about seven sleepyheads got up early to start building blockades, and the convoy of the establishment arrived early, too. One older cop came forward to check us out. He was friendly and easy to talk to, which surprised me. I found myself chatting without fear. Next thing I knew he was moving away from me, scribbling into a notepad, clearly writing down something I'd said.

> Never trust a cop, don't answer their questions, and never ever snitch.
>
> —*Direct Action Manual*

After the usual business of standing aside and watching silent men clear away the logs, we followed them to the falling zone. This time the tree-sitters answered our calls. Alex, a musician who had sung at the demo back in Vancouver in front of the Fletcher building, sang songs as police hung around.

The video-cop was getting on everyone's nerves. I saw him attempt to turn someone's face toward him. "Don't touch me!" she cried, running away. He denied touching her at all, with these words: "You're lying, young lady. I know better."

A handful of us hiked to the cutblock to support the tree-sitters. Two foremen were there alone, telling us the company had gone for lunch. We clambered through the slash and had a shouted conversation with our sitters. The foremen then warned us that logging would continue in five minutes. It did not.

Tree-sitters, clearly, are effective; Fletcher kept going elsewhere to log. Imagine: if there were enough sitters, logging couldn't continue anywhere.

After the Stein Festival I decided to return to Kaxi:ks. On the way, I showed Pete and Max Mayne Island, where I spent summer vacations as a child and where a few family members were still living. I had heard from blockader Deb Cranberry about the latest poor sods to be arrested. There was Fred from Amsterdam, whose tree platform was destroyed by loggers who took chainsaws to it, forcing him down to the hands of waiting police.

And there was Green, not his real name, but the man who drove me and countless others to the blockade site every day. I hadn't mentioned him in my journals even, for fear of whose hands those pages might fall into, but I was falling for him. I wasn't likely to see him again in the valley, though, thanks to his arrest.

I had been distracted by this crush during the final days of my first sojourn at camp. I hadn't wanted to fess up to anyone. But my new friend Jodi lured me to her trailer one day, and we holed up in there to gossip. She told me she had "the hots" for Wild Man John. "Oh, his chest!" she sighed, and in the same breath explained she was Buddhist and believed all desire leads to suffering. She was committed to being an observer.

John was a real loner, always going off on his own, mysteriously. His clothes were *olde worlde*—no jeans or T-shirts, but romantic flowy blouses and tattered vests. He was usually barefoot, with a colourful Celtic knot tattoo on one foot, and several toenails carved in knotwork, too. In England, he lived in a bus. We'd seen pictures of the inside of it. Everything was carved or painted in Celtic knotwork, even the wooden handle of the sink pump and a stained glass window.

Jodi reflected: "You can't pin a guy like that down. He's paranoid about someone controlling him. He's been chased by women all his life and he's tired of it. He prefers loneliness. He sits with safe women—those who are already in a relationship or those who are obviously not looking for one."

At the time, I was impressed by her analysis, but later John got together with the woman who painted my face. I was in awe of her, too, so I wasn't surprised. She had long red hair and clothes rather like his.

It was in the trailer that I confessed to Jodi my admiration for Green, and not without discomfort. He wore long sleeves in the hottest weather, usually a tattered old purple mac shirt. Didn't want the sun on his skin. He wore nerdy sweat pants and runners. I never saw him in the water. Three, maybe four years my senior, he spoke softly and didn't act macho. We shared a hug when I left, and he wanted to know if I would return. Soon I would be there again, but he would not. My main love interest was, of course, the rainforest. How could I think of anything but defending it? Everything in my life must help me to preserve Earth and her creatures, I felt. It could be no chore, no drudgery. Loving the world was heaven.

I said goodbye to Max. He and Pete were to spend a day on Galiano Island, then Max would leave from there for Vancouver. His flight to Blighty was next day. Good old Max kept us in hysterics. Actually, they were a pretty good double act.

It was consoling to remember that the course of study I'd soon be taking was about practical conservation, traditional rural skills, improving farmland to encourage prolific wildlife, and so on, in the countryside of Shropshire. It wouldn't be blockading, but it would be useful.

Before all of that, however, my world turned upside down on August 15. Pete and I made it back to Kaxi:ks, and it was being plundered. Upon our arrival, we were warmly welcomed by our new friends. But what had been like home was now the falling zone. Earlier, police had forced the move of base camp to the parking lot in front of the bridge. All other tents had to be moved away, at least as far as Emerald Pool. Any unclaimed tent was picked up and carried out by police. Was *this* legal? Were they ashamed of doing such work for Fletcher Challenge? Two cops—one male, one female—stood by me to make sure I took down my tent. I was upset and ranting.

"It's long past time we stopped making a living out of raping the earth," I fumed, yanking up pegs. "There are better ways."

The woman remarked, "You guys are paranoid." But the guy looked like he had never heard or thought of anything like this before.

A man who had cemented himself into the road was removed easily because even though he had been there all night, the cement had never completely dried. Even as I frantically recorded everything in my journal, everyone was crying. Ten of us were cut off from the rest of the camp; we were past the Pool, so the bridge divided us. The falling zone divided us.

We weren't going to be dealt with politely anymore. I guessed company orders were to force a way through. The ten of us didn't have much food and didn't know what was happening. I did hear one piece of sad news, though. They had already taken the guardian cedar snag with its platform, the one that spoke to Jodi, telling her: "If I go, we'll all go." I was glad I hadn't been there to watch. Would they take Cubby's Tree, the mammoth elder four-cedars-in-one? Would they get farther in—would they take Maxine's Tree? (As of 2024, Maxine's Tree still lives, and two children's books about it remain popular.)

The forest was full of cops watching us. Guarding the zone, working for the company. The chainsaws wouldn't stop. We were not organized; people were tired and burnt out. There could be no more training for tree-sitting because the equipment was gone. Just then, a tree fell extremely near to us. Then, a blast rent the air.

It was clear that from now on, actions must be carried out at night, before 4:00 a.m. Sitters would have to be better prepared. To avoid early arrest, they'd have to be securely ensconced in their trees long before police turned up. And they might have to stay up for days at a time, which could be very uncomfortable. I had heard of sitters in Australia staying up for weeks at a time. (This was before two young men stayed in Tofino's Eik Cedar for thirty-five days, and before Julia Butterfly Hill lived in a California redwood for 738 days.) But unless loggers knocked down more platforms, sitting was the only effective way of postponing the destruction for any amount of time. And we didn't have that many sitters.

Wild Man John was having a hard time. Everything he built, they destroyed: benches, platforms, and benders. The latter were shelters made from tarpaulin-covered frames of flexible cedar branches in long rows and bent into upside down U shapes. They smashed it all. It was like they were destroying him, bit by bit. He expressed anger and grief by doing somersaults, not by being aggressive.

Would we be forced to retreat deeper and deeper into the forest each day? It didn't feel safe being cut off from the others. But logging finished for the day at 1:00 p.m. Utter relief. We were free to go where we pleased. Of course, every one of us went to view the damage. We had to climb over cut trees to reach the bridge. The trailhead had been buried. It wasn't so easy to get from camp to Emerald Pool anymore. When I came across the old snag, I just stood there. It didn't make sense that it was horizontal.

Where the kitchen used to be, Cain and John made a giant bonfire for the hell of it, or maybe to ease their feelings. It was a lot of work to put it out, just a few of us with buckets doing it. Cain had only recently joined camp. If any woman said something he didn't like, he hissed at her: "*Lilith.*"

When at last the fire was extinguished, I gratefully immersed myself in the river.

The next morning three sitters managed to scale their trees in time. But the police gave them a new surprise: a second charge. Until then, a person was charged with contempt of court when arrested, so if a sitter stayed up a tree, she or he was free, since cops would not climb to make the arrest. Now they charged such activists with resisting arrest, unless they came down immediately. One woman had been away from the area for a while and didn't know about the change; upon returning to the bridge, she was shocked at the sight of the new cutblock and hastily decided to go up a tree. As a result, she had hardly any gear and was too uncomfortable to stay up long. Her arrest was unfortunate.

The loggers deliberately felled every tree that had held a sitter. What could we do? At least we had delayed them. They spent the rest of the day road building in another area. It was easy to focus on the negative, on the losses, on the devastation. But for all we knew, without the blockades the company might have razed everything right down to the shore of Emerald Pool. We just didn't know.

Some of Fletcher's equipment had been vandalized, and not by us. The substance used was toxic; nobody who cared for the forest would bring that stuff in. But we were not to be trusted. Three security guards were now living at the bridge in their vehicles. Platforms had been built as they watched; not once did they intervene or say anything. It would have been easy to relax our vigilance in their presence. I wondered to whom they reported.

Somebody made a lovely meal at a new supersized bender. Friday night's meeting, although facilitated by Lyne, was dominated by men, and most of the talk dealt with feelings of general paranoia and suspicions that we were being infiltrated. At the end of it, we hadn't achieved much at all, having made only rough plans for Saturday. I wasn't even certain what those were. One newspaper article called us "a bunch of pinkos and unwashed ragamuffins."

Lying in our sleeping bags under the tarp-and-branch dome, several of us released tension by singing absolute nonsense at the top of our lungs. I had never seen Pete let loose before, and I was gobsmacked by his wild, loud silliness. In the end I could no longer sing, I was laughing so hard, rolling convulsively back and forth until I began to hack and cough.

The next morning there were thirty cars. Dozens of new people had poured into camp for a special gathering of forest protectors. (Maybe we were a threat after all.) I took Debra and her daughter Sasha, who had come from Salt Spring, to see the falls; they were not safe to swim in now due to strong currents and the rising of the river, leftovers from a wild storm that hit when I was away. The entire kitchen had been swept off the bank and down the river. We were still able to swim in Emerald, though. The water was colder. That night, big bonfires lit up either side of the bridge.

Debra's husband Chris brought me a piece of mail that turned out to be a disguised love letter from Green. On Sunday morning I was about to steal away to read it, when its author stood before me. He was nervous, because he was in the valley illegally, post-arrest. We stole away together, into the forest, behind a tree, and into each other's arms—only to get swarmed by mosquitoes! Soon, he had to catch a lift out.

Preparing to leave the Walbran, I tried and failed to put my emotions aside. I shared in one group hug and left small gifts for friends. Lyne walked with me along the trail. She suddenly decided she wanted a photo, and as she ran back to get her camera, I was left alone in my favourite spot. I heard logging machinery in the distance. The trees framed Emerald, the direction I'd just come from. I tried to freeze the image in my mind, so it would be there when I was groping for something in the dark, and when I was far away in Blighty, in the middle of exams, I could remember these times and be reminded to continue participating in whatever way humanly possible.

Lyne came back and took my picture. She gave me a shell necklace she had made. She came with me as far as the bridge and then the air horn blew, signalling police presence (yes, even on a Sunday). Lyne had already been arrested and was banned from the valley, so she had to run and hide immediately. Debra put her arm around me and walked me to my ride. I wanted to turn around and get arrested, but I'd be gone by the time my court date came up. I had to be patient. My college course in England would last a mere ten months.

I didn't get to say goodbye to Pete. He was in the middle of a tree-climbing workshop.

Green visited me in North Van before I left the country. He brought an issue of Victoria's daily *Times Colonist* that showed a picture of a logger holding a cigarette in his clenched fist and, with his other hand, pinning a blockader to a tree by the neck.

We watched another new friend's arrest on the news. Police carried him out of his bender. The company was about to begin blasting the road through, directly above Emerald Pool. Fletcher Challenge could even get a blanket injunction, making it illegal for anyone to be within thirty kilometres of active logging. If they did, base camp would have to come down for good.

Blockades and arrests continued into September, by which time there were twenty-one charges of contempt of court. Subsequent trials resulted in fines and community hours. Fletcher Challenge was suing arrestees. Kathy, one of the five Torontonian women, fell from a tree, broke her back, and spent nine months in hospital. Our gang visited her, and they made a little video for me. Kathy has lived with the pain all this time. No one should have to go through that. Tree climbing, with proper gear and training, is a serious undertaking. It's worth looking into why mistakes happen, but not worth looking for blame. We didn't have what Clayoquot had the following summer: an organization already thirteen years running. In fact, North America may have been ahead on activist tree climbing, because when Pete and John taught a workshop on it at England's Glastonbury Festival, they were swamped with excited participants, and tree occupations in Blighty seemed to snowball after that.

The family of nine children and their parents lived on in the Kaxi:ks valley for four years. One person continued even longer to live in, collect information on, and fight for the forest. Various deferrals on different parts of the valley have come and gone, as has the continued logging.

This is a good spot to share words from retired logger Jim Gillespie, interviewed in 1991 for *The Road Stops Here*, a half-hour film by Heather Frise, Velcrow Ripper, and Barb Turner, which is easily viewed on YouTube.

"There isn't a logger today who can pass his cork boots on to his children. Not one of 'em! Y'know. Cuz there's only a few years left. They remove it so quickly. They take it out so fast. It's 'get rich, pull out.' … Six hunded thousand acres a year! … Grapple yarders, excessive road building, smashin' 'n' rippin' 'n' tearin'. In ten years, our economy is gonna be up against a wall here. I've cut down trees that were two thousand years old. A fourteen foot cedar, solid right through! No kidding. And when that thing went down … like a small earthquake. … I got an hour's wages outta that. And it took two thousand years to grow. That tells me somethin'. That I don't think we're gonna see any of this again."

ƛAʔUUKWIIʔATḤ, SUMMER 1992

Even though I'd been busy in England, I had also been in preparation. While the British media was full of the Christmas collapse of the Soviet Union, I'd steal into the dark college library to watch *The Road Stops Here*, which I must have somehow acquired on VHS, and which Green must have converted to UK format. Much as I loved rural Shropshire's countryside, it was not a threatened original ecosystem supporting millions of species and helping to control the planet's climate.

Journal entry, Wednesday, July 28. "I'm writing this at an action camp near Tofino, on the middle of the west coast of Vancouver Island, just past a bridge over Clayoquot Arm, a long extension of Kennedy Lake. I've been watching shrews, chipmunks, red-shafted flickers, one bald eagle, a pair of great blue herons perched high in two trees, dragonflies, bluets, and river otters. The threatened area is known as Clayoquot Sound. It's a lot bigger and more complex than the Walbran; it contains many different mountains, rivers, basins, channels, and estuaries. The group organizing the blockade is Friends of Clayoquot Sound (FOCS). I'm here because the blockade is here. Clearcutting is clearcutting. This time the corporation is MacMillan Bloedel."

Green had already been to the new camp. Instead of a freezing, rushing river, we were tenting next to a lake. Our location did not mark the end of a logging road meeting with the edge of the rainforest; the road continued past us all the way up a mountain. And this year's site was in marginal, mature forest, with some second growth (planted after being logged in the 1970s). I missed Max and Pete, but there were plenty of interesting people to meet. The tent I shared with Green was, to my joy, under a big old cedar. Red alder was everywhere, a land healer.

"You must be the woman Green visited in England twice in ten months." his friends said to me when we were introduced.

"Yes," I smiled back. Back then, airplane pollution and climate change didn't occur to us as much as it does now. "Once for Christmas and once for spring break." During the latter, we had joined Pete, Bee, Maggie, Corinne, Mac, and Wild Man John on his bus. While we toured around rain-soaked Ireland, Max was at home working on Canterbury archaeological digs and tending his animal sanctuary in Herne Village, Kent.

This summer the loggers would often find the Clayoquot Arm bridge empty, but a tall, imposing barricade—made of beams from an older bridge—greeted them farther along the road. The banner on top stated: STOP CLEARCUTS. ANCIENT RAINFORESTS FOREVER, NOT JUST TOKEN GROVES.

FOCS had been active since 1979. It was formed to protect Meares Island, or Wanačis-Hiłthuuʔis. The island's elevations, Lone Cone (Wanačis) and Mount Colnett (Hiłthuuʔis), make up part of the ancestral and unceded lands of two local Indigenous nations. These mountains also form a gorgeous vista for Tofino. Community members voluntarily rose to action when there was a threat to the forests of Meares, and joined Tlaoquiaht Elected Chief Moses Martin in preventing MacMillan Bloedel from landing on the island with chainsaws. (Read more about this in the epilogue.) FOCS members had already been imprisoned for blocking logging at Sulphur Pass back in 1988. The Friends' policy statement read:

1. To promote the protection of all remaining temperate rainforest in Clayoquot Sound.

2. To promote the cessation of clear-cut logging practices.

3. To ensure that restoration occurs on all lands and waters in Clayoquot Sound which have been degraded.

4. To support self-determination for aboriginal peoples.

5. To promote bioregionalism.

   [According to *Cascadia Field Guide*, "A bioregion is defined by the characteristics of the natural environment rather than by Human-made divisions—essentially, a 'life place.' … Bioregionalists know that Humans and our cultures are part of nature, not apart from it, and we should focus our efforts on building sustainable relationships within our sociological and ecological environments."]

I attended several nonviolent civil disobedience workshops. During role play, one activist portrayed an obnoxious TV reporter to whom individuals had to answer tricky on-the-spot questions without time to think ahead. It was good practice for the use of sound bites—brief statements suitable for television news.

Reporter: "Are you a member of Earth First!"

Answer: "To me the Earth does come first, certainly before profits, or else the human race dies; however, I am not a member of any group by that name."

Earth First!, in fact, never had a recorded membership, although one could subscribe to the *Earth First! Journal*. The media and Mac Blo seemed to be trying to drum up a link between the Friends and the US-based direct-action monkeywrenching group. But Earth First! promoted illegal deeds like tree-spiking and messing with logging machinery, while the Friends didn't participate in those kinds of activities. They wanted the media to focus on clearcutting rather than accusations.

Next, we formed a "hassle line" in pairs. One partner would play a logger, the other an environmentalist, while a potentially nasty confrontation was enacted. The environmentalist needed to calm the logger down with well-spoken arguments. Not an easy task.

LOGGER: What the hell are you doing here? I've got a family to feed!

ACTIVIST: I know. I'm not here to take your job away from you. I'm here to stop clearcutting because I'm worried about future generations being able to feed their families, and—

LOGGER: You are taking my job!

ACTIVIST: Isn't it mechanization that's taking your job away?

LOGGER: Are you on welfare?

ACTIVIST: No, I took time off work because I'm so concerned about this. And I wouldn't begrudge someone on welfare to act for the forests. Clearcutting is devastating the land and rivers! If we continue at this rate your job will be over in five to ten years anyway, right?

LOGGER: How do *you* know? I've got to think about today! My kids have to be fed.

ACTIVIST: Of course they do. You and I have a common struggle against the big companies. The bosses hide in their offices pulling all the strings while you and I face each other on the road.

Throughout the exercise, activists and loggers interrupted each other, often yelling, the loggers usually swearing. It was good practice. The class difference had to be faced. Loggers were workers, doing what they knew how to do to bring in money, and a lot of us were more fortunate or privileged. Not all, but many. On the other hand, most of us had pathetic incomes compared to a logger's. What about the difference in either of our incomes and that of Mac Blo's CEO? Anyway, it was paper buyers we should have also been talking to. Who was using old-growth timber, where were these trees ending up? That would come later.

To reduce the adrenaline, there was a presentation on the history of land protection in Clayoquot Sound. What I found most interesting was the history of Indigenous and non-Indigenous people uniting to protect Meares. The Tlaoquiahts declared that island a Tribal Park. The colonial court didn't recognize their declaration, but no chainsaws dared return.

Finally, consensus was explained. Most of us were fairly ignorant regarding alternative ways of group planning and decision making. In theory, no action could or would go ahead without everyone feeling okay about it. There was no voting. It was about offering a forum for communication that encouraged both listener and speaker in all of us.

One morning at the blockade, we laid logs and boulders in front of the bridge. Behind them we walked in a circle, holding our placards and chanting. Farther along the road, a man called Noah was padlocked to the gate. I felt a degree of responsibility for him. We had chatted the night before, and he had said he wasn't willing to get arrested. When I rambled off some of my reasons for wanting

Painting signs in Mark Hobson's backyard, Tofino, 1992. Valerie Langer is seated in the centre with bare feet. Photo: Mark Hobson

to be arrested, he said my words made him reconsider. Now, U-lock around his neck, he shrugged and smiled at my open mouth.

As workers were cutting Noah from the gate, activists who were watching suddenly shouted that he was being choked. Then the long pole that was holding up our banner came down, hitting two of our people and one logger. Other employees of MB showed no concern whatsoever. Nor did the police.

We all crowded in, concerned for Noah's safety. This angered an irritable, tank-sized cop, who ordered us to stand aside or face arrest. He had previously promised that the arrestee's support person, Dan, would not be arrested himself. This promise was suddenly broken. Dan was naturally horrified and angry. He immediately went limp, shouting about the injustice as they carried him away. Then he was weeping. I was sure this scene would make the news, and that the police would wish it hadn't. It was a possibility that Dan's history of arrests was their reason for taking him this time. They knew he would likely receive a heavier sentence.

Before the paddy wagon had a chance to drive off, a large black bear decided to cross the bridge in our direction. Everyone, including media with video cameras, excitedly moved toward it. It—she? he?—was beautiful, with thick, glossy fur. With humans closing in, the bear became frightened and started to run. I thought I could see the bridge shaking under the animal's feet. Everyone froze as it reached the end—our end. Clearly scared, it leaped into the bushes, crashing away out of sight.

During the circle afterwards, a loon flew overhead uttering its haunting cry. Another good omen from the wild. The animals gave us needed encouragement, especially when fallers called us "scum."

A bunch of us drove to the cutblock later. Clearcuts scarred the land all the way up the mountain, contrasting with panoramic views of the valley below, part of which was blanketed under a thick snow-white mist. As sunshine started to melt it, the full length of Clayoquot Arm was revealed. A logging truck full of giant trees rumbled past us, stirring up billows of dust.

Green took me to Tofino for the first time. As many Indigenous folk as settlers and tourists walked around the small downtown. Some lived in Tofino, but most lived on reservations, the same as today. Their village of Opitsat is situated just across the harbour on Wa-načis-Hiłthuuʔis. People have been living on that spot for thousands of years.

From Tofino I could only see one or two clearcuts and they were old, not raw. A view like that was rare then, even rarer now. But would I want to settle here? Green was keen. So many environ-mentalists! That's what Tofino was to us: an activist's mecca. Surf-ing was entirely irrelevant. But I'd been moving around for so long, the idea of settling anywhere was, well, unsettling. And we knew about the seasonal housing shuffle, or had heard about it: monthly rentals were available for locals only until the spring, when tourism resumed. This would worsen over the decades when winter's re-spite disappeared to make way for year-round short-term vacation rentals.

Back on the logging road the next morning there were more arrests, one of which, unfortunately, was a support person again. At first, I was busy watching a cameraperson's back, because yesterday a logger had grabbed and shoved him. After a while I joined the circle in the middle of the road. We decided to form a Council of All Beings: going clockwise, each person spoke as a forest animal, plant, or even valley or mountain or river. My new friend Maryjka's turn came and she began: "I am the Clayoquot River valley—" and burst into tears. I was Coyote, because this animal has been persecuted as "vermin" for so long. (I found out later there aren't any coyotes on Vancouver Island. Embarrassing.) Jean McLaren, one of the Raging Grannies (a movement of activist singing groups in flower-laden hats), was in costume as Mother Earth. I wondered how the arresting officers felt as they led this white-haired lady away. George, a seventeen-year-old, went limp and was carried off. It was his support person who was also arrested. The young and the old making a stand! Ours was a broad-based movement, not to be conveniently labelled as kids, hippies, or "welfare bums" standing alone.

My own arrest took place on Friday, July 31, 1992. Our plan was to erect a mast-like structure over the middle of the bridge with someone hanging from it in a harness. This seemed more elaborate than a tripod—which was used in the Walbran after I'd left—but carried the same point: occupation by a person out of cops' reach. People had stayed up all night working on it, and apart from the guy who was to sit in it, I was that day's only planned arrestee. Things sure turned out differently: twenty-six people were arrested.

There was disappointment all around when the structure immediately broke due to a truck driver accidentally towing the rope too fast, too soon.

I ended up lying across the bridge within a ring of stones, wearing a homemade papier mâché bear mask over my head, and holding a poster of a landslide caused by an MB clearcut. We wanted to remind people of the animals being irreversibly affected by this kind of logging. It was that bear who had so recently run across the bridge whose habitat was (and is) disappearing, after all.

A banner, spread out on the bridge next to me, said BRITISH COLUMBIA: BRAZIL OF THE NORTH. This was meant to state how BC forest practices were as bad as Brazil's destruction of the Amazonian rainforest. The process server read the injunction to me while a protector simultaneously read aloud the UN Resolution on Biodiversity. I did not reply when asked to move; bears can't speak for themselves. The police were a long time in coming anyway.

Sometimes I was too warm, but mostly I was freezing as I lay there, visualizing myself hugging the big cedar by my tent. What if I were a real dead bear, lying across the bridge? Would they stop then? If a logging truck or crummy hit a bear along the road, was that a war casualty? What if logging or yarding or blasting destroyed a bear's den, or buried a bear alive? (This is what motorway extensions did to badgers in England until the Badger Watch groups became active.)

I could see next to nothing with the mask on. Where was Green? There was a large banner between myself and the circle. My support person, Lisa, told me there were fifty people, and I wondered where they had all come from. She informed me that most had come from Tofino—the local residents taking a stand for the rainforest. In the end, half were apprehended.

I heard cheers of names and thanks as each person was dragged away. The police were apparently selective in who they took. For example, an elderly woman, Sue from Port Alberni, stood for hours in the middle of the road, right in front of an MB truck.

"She looked like the quintessential old granny," said Valerie. "She spoke sweetly and softly. Her white hair, beige trench coat, purse, and comfortable soft-soled loafers made her the least 'hippie' looking person ever. And yet her determination to come out from Port—a logging town where she was sure to face real backlash from her neighbours—was the epitome of the courage of ordinary people in extraordinary times."

Ignored by police, Sue repeatedly asked officers why they weren't arresting her. When they finally did, she was not charged. Yet others who were off to the side of the road were deliberately taken and charged. It had to have been because they were known activists, whereas a second senior (Sue, along with Jean the day before) would definitely suggest an all-ages movement to the public. And frankly, arresting grandmothers looked bad.

Some arrests, as I learned later, were entirely unplanned, unexpected, and unwanted. Most, on the other hand, were spontaneous actions taken by people who decided, on the spot, that they would not move aside for the destruction. I was shivering and thinking about pancakes when shouts of horror reached my ears: a scene of hair pulling was taking place that would air later on television. Someone's daughter sobbed, "Don't take my daddy away!"

After the noise died down, Lisa appeared at my ear and described the scene to me. Rather than arrest the grandmother, the police grabbed FOCS board member and past arrestee Julie Draper.

This was when it dawned on defenders that organizers were targeted. A group of people responded by sitting down on the road and linking arms and legs. This was Painter Jim, Derek Shaw, Eric, Rob Flemming and his partner Shari Bondy, and an Australian man. The cops tried to unlock this knot of people by inflicting pain: grabbing, pulling, pushing, bending back fingers, and digging into pressure points. One of the cops leaned over, locked eyes with Derek, and slow-motion punched him in the face. A threat. Then the hair pulling began.

I lay silently fuming. We were citizens of Earth, doing our duty through nonviolent civil disobedience. We were not criminals, although Mac Blo, Crown counsel, and a judge were conspiring to make most of the trials criminal—rather than civil—contempt of court. If they were criminal cases, the taxpayer, rather than MB, forked out for legal fees. It was sickening how much power a logging company had.

Small white clouds moved slowly across the blue sky in my eye holes. Condensation was beginning to form inside the mask. But each time the paddy wagon filled up and drove off I could relax, sit up, and take it off. I spotted Green, busy taking photographs. I was not abandoned. Lisa brought me pancakes and painkillers. And an American guy who claimed to be the star employee for Subway sandwiches in Seattle graced us with his presence.

I'll call him Mick. He wasn't crazy about me, because I let it slip that I didn't care for the Rolling Stones. Mick wore a poncho, shorts, socks that didn't match, and a beret on his head. He sang famous songs, changing the lyrics to suit the blockade, which made Lisa and me laugh. Freddie Mercury had died the previous November, and Mick sang "Another One Bites the Dust" for every arrest. He wrote a eulogy for me—for the Dead Bear. It consisted of as many different Shakespearean quotes as he could recall, each one suitably altered to include trees, clearcuts, and so forth. Mick wanted to read it as I was being carried away. Everyone warned him to stand aside when the time came, but when the cops appeared he stood right over me.

"Are you going to move, sir?"

"Yeah, but I just want to read this eulogy first—hey! Wait!"

He had bitten the dust. He was under arrest.

I lay still and saw several cops moving to and fro through my eye holes. One of them spoke:

"Should we take the bear now?"

I should have roared. I went blank. I'm not even sure if they asked me whether I'd move. They pulled off the mask and I was dragged, a cop on each arm. I was not one of the lucky ones who got one cop for each limb. The officer on my left was gripping extremely hard. Then they dropped me for a minute. I was sitting up with my head bent down. I sensed Green nearby; we didn't speak. I heard a woman say to her child, "Mama Bear is very tired." I smiled. As he was taking my arm again, a policeman said angrily, "This is a wonderful thing for a child to see." The woman retorted, "It's a wonderful thing for you to do, sir."

I did not feel like I could go willingly from the destruction of the planet, so again I was painfully dragged. A video camera chased me and I wondered why I wasn't shouting anything to the BC premier or the world like I had planned. They tossed me into a police car and shut the door. I was on my back with my legs in the air next to a woman I knew.

"Hi," she said.

"Hi." I was glad to see her.

I got right side up and emptied my boots of rubble. My forearm was burning and she felt it.

"That's really hot!"

It was sore. I pulled my sleeve up and saw red speckly marks; all the skin on my armpit was peeled and hanging. It stung for a long time.

During the drive to Ucluelet police station, the cop made conversation with my companion, using her first name as if they were old friends. She was, after all, a well-known activist. He ignored me.

As we arrived at the police station, he said the processing could take six hours. I admit, my heart sank. We walked past a full paddy wagon into the garage. Men and women were immediately separated. I was led into a small cell where, to my relief, I recognized two of the five women. All of them sat on two bunks looking at one seatless, steel toilet, a tiny sink, and me, menstruating. I was still waiting for painkillers to kick in, and I felt like hell—tired and hungry on top of the cramps.

When it was my turn to be processed, the RCMP desk riders kept asking if I was a Canadian citizen. I guess they thought I was British (I still spoke with a hint of accent after living there for four years before the Walbran blockade, then returning for another year). They noticed my tattoo and made a note of it. My eyes were closed in the mugshot, but the photographer didn't bother trying for a better picture. At least they didn't take my fingerprints! They did remove my necklace, bracelets and brooch, and asked for my earrings and even my hair wrap. I refused. (The hair wrap would have had to be cut from my head, and the earrings were hell to deal with.) My leopard-spotted cotton menstrual pad distracted the plods while I hid my best wristband in my underwear. They claimed they'd only ever seen disposables. Everything was returned as soon as we were released anyway, which was far less than the threatened six hours. It was more like two.

As I signed the form, I heard my name. I turned around—and there were all the arrested men, a whole garage full, waving and making peace signs through a window.

Later, inside the cell, I knocked on the door to ask for my pad back. Instead of the usual woman answering, a little old man answered. At least, he seemed old to my twentysomething self. When I explained I was bleeding heavily he looked shocked and exclaimed, "Really?" All the women burst out laughing. The man quickly went and came back with the pad, closing the door after himself gently and carefully.

Maybe that had something to do with why I was let go first. To be released, I had to sign a form promising to stay five kilometres away from active logging operations. Sitting at the sergeant's desk, I found my hands were shaking. I showed him my torn armpit, but his eyes reflected only ridicule; he stated that it was my fault for not going willingly. The fact that I did not resist arrest but went limp, in the tradition of nonviolence, was not something I bothered to point out to him. I wondered if he thought the Indian police were right to club Gandhi over the head when he made this peaceful method of protest famous. "It is as important to disobey unjust laws as it is to obey just laws," Gandhi said.

Finally, I was let into the waiting room where a few people waited for various arrestees. I got a hug from a woman I didn't even know. She was waiting for her husband, who had sat behind me on the bridge. The toddler who had been crying for her daddy was their daughter, Divina. I went outside and wandered around until I spotted Green asleep in his vehicle.

That night, CBC's eleven o'clock news showed us getting dragged off and I was glad my supportive, worried grandmother somehow missed it over in North Vancouver. BCTV news showed plenty of police brutality, including a very unnerving shot of someone being pulled away by his hair. Why was I surprised? Did I think Canadian police would be gentler than the Brits with their clubs? I believed the police would have been happy with a riot; they claimed we were the violent ones. They called us terrorists!

Many people, myself among them, planned to file official complaints. I saw several injuries apart from my own skinned armpit. After that, people from all over the province called in to the Friends of Clayoquot Sound's office to express shock and anger at the police violence. My journal says that not only were the police and MB surprised to find protectors after that day (they thought they'd cleaned us out), but they were under strict new orders to be peaceful. I don't remember how I or FOCS came by this information, or who gave those orders, but it was a comfort.

⁂

Even though I couldn't legally blockade anymore, I was in the loop when volunteering for the Friends. Nearly every journal entry recorded how many people were arrested each morning. Eight on August 4, four the next day, and so on. Not many, and yet they accumulated. In a Ucluelet lawyer's office, I applied for legal aid with two other arrestees. We all qualified financially but because it was our first offence, the head office in Vancouver wouldn't cover us, since (they reasoned) all we were likely to get was a slap on the wrist. To our relief, the Victoria branch covered us.

While in "Ukee" (the local nickname for Ucluelet), we noticed the *Sea Shepherd* anchored in the harbour. The ship was as black as a bear, with a deliberate pirate vibe. Sea Shepherd was and is a direct-action organization that puts its neck on the line with risky confrontations. Its crews go out into the open sea and ram whaling vessels, or sink them when they're docked. Greenpeace had started this in the early 1970s, challenging Soviet whaling boats from small dinghies. I didn't know what Sea Shepherd was doing in Ukee harbour. Humpback whales had been virtually gone from these waters (and have made a comeback during my decades on the island). There had been a moratorium on commercial whaling since 1982. Perhaps some of the crew were taking part in the blockades. It was a reminder that other things were happening, not only in the world but right here on the west coast.

Another day, we visited the Mac Blo forestry information centre in Tofino. Thereafter we called it the "disinformation centre." Each display was slickly done. MB had obviously been spending a lot of money on its public image. And it was on good terms with other companies; I found a paper published by Fletcher Challenge called "Managing the Walbran." It was made to look exactly like a Western Canada Wilderness Committee publication, only glossier. *Managing the Walbran.* The arrogance of colonialism. Like Pacheedaht-Qwabadiwa territory needed to be managed. Translation: mis-managed for profit and ruin. Stolen land, scraped raw.

Green and I visited nearby Pacific Rim National Park to walk in the "designated rainforest area." The path was covered by a boardwalk, and by wood chips in some places. This was to protect the sensitive soil and root systems from thousands of human shoes. The display boards dotting the route were informative and educational, but it felt a little like walking through a tree museum. This depressed me, even though I appreciated the effort to keep tourists in a handful of places so they (we) wouldn't invade every area. And the path was wheelchair accessible. But museums, I thought, displayed things that used to be. And they were known for stealing cultural artifacts. Future human generations should be able to enjoy real temperate rainforest, and future nonhuman animals will need a home. An ecosystem could never be contained within a museum. And parks? They are un-treatied, unceded Indigenous land and have, for the most part, been awarded their designation without the say or involvement of the descendants of their original ancestral caretakers.

A belted kingfisher flew through the forest. It had much duller plumage than a European kingfisher, was larger and not so quick. We joined a group led by a young Parks Canada employee who spoke about the cycles of growth in the rainforest. She enthused about the recycling of nutrients from fungi, dead standing trees, and nurse logs. Without the latter, there would be no forest!

We also attended a free film, *An Island of Whales*, which featured incredible footage of whales around Vancouver Island, with the usual sorrowful message of threatened extinction. In fact, after the movie when the warden stood up to show the audience a few whale bones, he asked, "Are these remains all that our grandchildren will know of the largest mammals on Earth?"

A mother bear and her two cubs cautiously crossed the highway in single file. The cubs kept looking back at us, but didn't run. Judging from the mother's medium size, the bear we saw at the blockade must have been a male.

❦

On August 6, 1992, no one stayed put for arrest; all stood aside to let the workers through instead. Everything was on video. But MB security engaged Tofino citizens in conversation on the bridge until two cops turned up. Then the tank-sized cop arrested the lot! Seven distressed people including a District of Tofino Council member and a schoolteacher. One woman struggled and argued as she was led to the paddy wagon, but the Tank was out of control and not listening. As he took each person, he said he was doing so simply because they were on the bridge. When one last woman tried to explain the group's innocence—the fact that they had all stood aside when asked—he stubbornly retorted, "What are you doing here?"

"Well, we're protesting the—"

"You're protesting? Then you're under arrest." The Tank may be the first officer in Canadian history to claim that simply protesting in this country is illegal. "I'm tired of babysitting you," he added.

"Um, I'm pretty sure this is the first time we've met?" someone said.

Sitting in the police van, the upset woman continued talking to him. She said she felt that MB's security guards had entrapped them by engaging them in conversation until police arrived. She even called out to the men and asked them if it was true.

"Don't be ridiculous," one of them replied.

The most interesting part for me was the image of the Tank waving his finger down at Nicole (who was a foot shorter than he), the only person he didn't arrest, telling her she was a nuisance. As if this tiny woman was physically impeding MB, even though she had moved aside. What a tête-à-tête! Sasquatch-sized bully mansplaining to a concerned mother that she was a threat and to mind her own business. He concluded, "If I see you again, I will arrest you." What obviously never occurred to the Tank was that Nicole was minding her business by wanting to protect the forest, if not by arrest, then by witnessing.

Down the logging road on the way to the station, the paddy wagon got a flat tire. All seven people were suddenly released without charge. Luckily, they got rides back to town from friends, or they would have been stranded miles from the highway.

I had to laugh when I saw the news that evening. There was the Tank, shaking an arrestee's umbrella like a chastising finger at the camera, warning the person behind it, and thousands of viewers: "*You* stay off the bridge."

Later that month I had to attend a dehumanizing court in Victoria. The judge sat above everybody. Two people sat subserviently below him taking notes. We all should have been sitting in a clearcut.

Discussion between judge and lawyers was difficult to hear, let alone understand. They spoke about us as if we were not there in the same room with them, yet our presence was huge: standing room only. The judge had a posh English accent and a patronizing, impulsive smile. He seemed amused at the unusual situation. Some people were opting to defend themselves.

When we weren't in court, we circled at the city hall. Our meeting seemed to go on too long, so we were relieved by the appearance of Merv Wilkinson and his wife. The elderly couple had sustainably, selectively logged the same small forest on Vancouver Island for decades.

Our group decided to walk to the Ministry of Forests, and at 10:30 a.m. we peacefully tried to enter. The security guard wouldn't admit us, even though it was a public building. Nevertheless, several activists let themselves in via the downstairs parking lot, and none of us would leave until the minister met with us. Meanwhile, we made a terrific display of new, large, laminated photographs of clearcuts, landslides and damaged rivers. We took over both sides of the street in front of the ministry. HONK IF YOU HATE CLEARCUTS. Many did. We handed out information to pedestrians, too. But who would face us from the Ministry of Forests? Well, the only person not on holiday was a woman who had been working there only two weeks and didn't know much. She promised us she would pass on our concerns.

I left the city to camp alone on Salt Spring Island. As I was setting up my tiny, one-person tent, clouds covered the entire sky except for a sliver that lay from end to end along the western horizon. A delicious wind rose up. As the setting sun moved down into the thin line of clear sky, it cast an ethereal light on the valley, altering the colour of needles and leaves and arbutus bark. The hair on the back of my neck prickled. The air seemed anticipatory. My hands fumbled as I hurried to take down my hammock. I stuffed it inside my pack, which I placed under a substantial fir tree. Then I returned to my tent and dived inside it. I watched the sky until the rain came and I had to zipper the fly. The rain pelted down like hailstones. Lightning flashed continuously, and thunder became so loud it drowned out the sound of the rain. The noise was like a chasm ripping open hard ground. I plugged my ears and burrowed under my sleeping bag. Lightning might strike a tree which could then fall on me, or strike the cliff above me and knock boulders loose. I tried to think of a mantra to chant for comfort until eventually, mercifully, the thunder died down, the rain lightened, and sleep crept over me.

In late August, I somehow made my way back to Kaxi:ks/Walbran. There was a blockade after all! I set up camp in the same spot I had shared with Max and Pete a year previously, under two giant, gorgeous cedars still standing. The mice were crazy: they scampered all over my site and got into my food. I was sure they were bum-sliding down my tent fly in the night, having a wild party. I dreamt of being in class, but the classroom was overrun by wolves and other wild things. The chaos and the wildness felt strangely contagious.

Despite the joy of return there was grief. Where a single trail once wound peacefully through the forest after the bridge, leading to Emerald Pool, there was now a logging road, branching one way to a pile of rubble, the other to a clearcut. I could actually see the road from Emerald Pool. There were new trails all over the place, including many half-finished boardwalks (these would protect the roots, of course, I knew). Piles of wood were strewn around everywhere, grey mould and flies infested old shit pits, the smell of human waste lingered, and there was loss of vegetation on tent sites—what once was leafy green now lay flat, worn and brown. The new road changed everything, of course. And road building continued a few valleys over. This is why it is so important to save wildlife habitat for its own sake and not only for wreckreation.

But the sunlight still glowed on thousands of moss-hung branches. Birds and frogs sang, fish and water boatmen thrived, a dipper dipped, squirrels scolded. There is something about the sight of a tiny squirrel effortlessly scaling a massive old-growth tree. Due to fire hazard, there was no logging. I was startled to find a mere trickle where last year's waterfalls showered anyone who stood under them. The water was that low. The valley had been without rain for some time.

I moved my camping spot to the banks of Emerald and took to sleeping in Lyne's hammock, she in mine, both of us under her bender. I dreamt about cereal boxes and punk gigs. During the day my head rang with *The Love Boat*'s theme song. Is that how my mind dealt with unaccustomed (but welcome) silence?

The Friends of Carmanah Walbran and other groups were linking with the Qwabadiwa people and supporting them in their struggle. The name "Carmanah" is apparently a colonized version of "Qwabadiwa." Saving the rainforests was and is a social, as well as an environmental, cause; forest destruction is an act of blatant disregard for that forest's Indigenous nation.

Mac Blo now had a twenty-four-hour guard on site, plus Fletcher Challenge employees drove down often. Sometimes a helicopter would land. A promotional video was being made for Fletcher, featuring the Walbran. It should have been called How Not to Treat a Forest, or We Are the Exploiters.

On a Monday morning the rain came, ending the fire hazard. As a result, loggers returned, only to be blockaded. I was in the area illegally since my Clayoquot arrest meant I couldn't go near active logging sites on the entirety of Vancouver Island. So I hid in a vehicle, watching and listening from a distance.

A platform supporting an activist was suspended under a small bridge in an area licensed to Mac Blo. A few protectors talked with some loggers. Ron, a police sergeant, stood around discussing and debating with our side for an hour. He was in the hot seat, but he obviously enjoyed it; everyone wanted to hear what he had to say.

"Where do the police fit in at a blockade?" someone demanded.

"Where do we fit in?" answered Ron. "It's the old story of the peacekeepers."

I wanted to yell from my hiding spot, "So why did they pull hair and bruise limbs at Clayoquot?"

"We are truly a neutral party," I heard him say. Several voices of dissent rose in response.

"There's good police and bad police in Canada," he said, as if it were perfectly understandable and an acceptable state of affairs.

A little later when the conversation had switched to logging, he said, "Guys are getting laid off because there are too many moratoriums on these places."

Uproar.

"That's not true," rose the loudest voice. "It's increased mechanization and higher rate of cut!"

"The companies are geared for maximum profit, not maximum employment," another voice cried. Ron tried to say something, but was drowned out. The louder voice continued, "If they can buy a machine to do the work ten men used to do, they will. There's your job loss. More trees are being cut now than ever before! I can't believe you buy that line! You sound like a PR man for the companies."

I couldn't make out anything in reply; too many people were talking at once. I watched as the sergeant grinned and gestured and spoke to the guy who had challenged him. Then he moved away and bent over the bridge, where presumably he could communicate with the person on the suspended platform. The crowd trickled over to him and I couldn't hear much more.

Around three o'clock, logging equipment was utilized to suspend Ron from the bridge so he could arrest the activist. Mac Blo's injunction for the Walbran had expired, and finally the cop had realized that there existed a current, up-to-date Fletcher injunction for the area. It didn't seem to matter that MB was the company being blockaded; the Fletcher injunction would do.

I stayed nearly a week, enjoying Lyne's company and warped sense of humour. I read to her as she rebuilt John's old bender, and we discussed what was read. She was concentrating on weaving two long cedar branches together and bending them into a U.

"The human race is like a cancer spreading over the globe," I mused.

"I don't agree with that at all," she replied, with some irritation. "Only some races of humanity are ruining it for everyone else. We wouldn't be here if we didn't belong here. And how can we feel positive and empowered enough to be activists if we don't respect ourselves as human beings?"

A warmth flooded through me. I lifted my hands to my face because they were tingling. It took a while to recognize relief, belonging. I won't say it was consistent for the next three decades, but it was a memory to reach for in bleak times.

That turned out to be my last journey to Kaxi:ks. It was far from where I lived. First, there was the five-hour drive. But I was more deterred by two bumpy additional hours on unpaved road through depressing clearcuts. Pete, Max, and Green all went back, though. While still in England, finishing his degree and living in a London squat, Pete organized actions for the forest from his borrowed desk at an Earth First! office. He helped construct a large old-growth cedar over a backpack frame, and carried it onto the London underground on his way to shutting down BC House.

In time, he immigrated to Canada. He and Lyne had a baby, Fern.

ƛAʔUUKWIIʔATḤ, AUTUMN 1992

I remember an evening in Tofino when we watched an eagle-shaped cloud floating in front of the mountains transform itself into the head of a dragon. The mountains were Lone Cone and Mount Colnett on Meares Island, which I've already mentioned is Wanačis-Hiłthuuʔis Tribal Park.

We spent that night at the bed and breakfast that would become our winter home in a few weeks.

Green's friend took us to Vargas Island on a sailboat for an eco-gathering. As the wind filled the sails, I lay on one of the nets (like a wide, tight hammock), enjoying the ride, gazing at the sun-speckled water over which we sped. In Ahousaht territory, tents of many colours had sprouted up on Yarksis beach, site of the former village Kelsemat. The distant islands and mountains showed no clear-cut scars and were covered in old growth, as they had been for thousands of years.

Members of Indigenous nations and activist groups strategized to develop more effective ways of working together for change. After two hours, I broke away to play with children and frisbees and dogs, running in and out of the water.

During the night, a storm blew up. I was grateful that I had brought new-to-me gumboots and a serious raincoat. In the morning, puny boats were taking crowds of people out onto the raging sea. I was clammy with fear. We had to wade through the whitecaps with our packs to reach the boat. The ocean poured through my rain gear and filled up my boots; I was in up to my waist and most of my pack was underwater. Green pulled me up and into the boat. It handled the waves well, but the spray and rain combined were gruelling, not to mention frigid. A child was wailing in misery. It seemed like ages before we reached First Street dock. We spent hours at the laundromat dropping coins into dryers. The highway was flooded until evening. I was starting to look forward to having a home.

While people met daily around tables in boardrooms, the trees were still falling. Tofino citizens wrote letters to various ministers, sending them via the Friends' fax machine so they would arrive fast. When I wrote to Premier Mike Harcourt this time, I was brief and emphasized the need for job alternatives and retraining. Decades later this is called a Just Transition. I sent copies to the minister of forests and the minister ofenvironment/parks. Of course, workers have to be on board with relearning. Bruce Hornidge, retired faller and author of *Loggerheads: A Memoir*, writes:

> Because we all expected to return to our normal employment [after a blockade], few of us wanted to commit to any very long-term training. Most of the emerging forestry employment positions required university degrees or qualifications that took years of study to achieve. Few of us felt young enough or motivated enough to pursue such avenues to a new career.

But I met loggers who did retrain. We have to green the economy without leaving anyone behind. It's survival.

Local activists began to stand outside Mac Blo disinformation centre with signs and counter-information. That usually caused the place to close early. We knew even then that temperate rainforests were the planet's climate control centres.

On the last night of September 1992, coming into Tofino we saw a tiny mouse scramble across the highway as fast as it could go, followed by a hopping frog. When we finally slowed down in front of our new home—Raven's Haven B&B—we saw what appeared to be a wolf. Large and white in the headlights, with glowing green eyes, it moved along the path on our side while keeping a wary eye on us, then quickly crossed the road to disappear into the forest like a ghost. When in England, driving at night I always hoped to see a fox, badger, hedgehog, or polecat. In Tlaoquiat, I realized that the highway itself was a mere path through habitat that loomed up on either side, where wolves, bears, deer, and cougars lived. The England I knew had flattened corpses on country lanes and highways. I didn't know about country lanes anywhere in BC, but Pacific Rim Highway seemed to have very few roadkills. There was more room for creatures to move around without having to go near a road, though on a peninsula they would encounter water.

Raven's Haven was surrounded by dense forest which reached all the way to the edges of bays and sandy beaches. I confess to expressing disgust that anyone in Tofino would own and watch television. I had lived with a four-channel TV in England, but here? Surely this place was too beautiful to want to look anywhere but outside. I had, after all, already missed the first several seasons of *Star Trek: The Next Generation*.

At Mackenzie Beach—proper name Tin Wis—a small island was connected by sandbar to the rest of the beach; one had to know the tides before exploring. Storm-worn trees were hung with hairy lichen. Old cedars produced huge tangled masses of curving branches like elephant trunks. The long green slugs were also worth admiring. I stepped over little messes, either of scat or food. Now I reckon they were river otter, raccoon, or mink droppings.

This was the first autumn I'd spent in Canada for five years, and at first I was missing colourful deciduous trees. Nearly everything in Tofino stays green all year round. But I looked forward to a green winter. A new friend, Sara Jane, phoned and invited us to go on a hike from Radar Hill—proper name Naćaas, pronounced Nats'aas—to the beach below it. We took Sid along, one of the dogs from our new home. On the hilltop we admired a panoramic view, so unabused, so uninterrupted, so unlike England's patchwork quilt. A bald eagle soared past us, its brown and white body striking against the green.

It has now been many years since I tried that trail. I recall it being nearly vertical in some places, extremely rooty, and always muddy. There were jungles of ferns, and swampy patches wound around by a few gurgling streams. That first time there were many mushrooms and other fungi of chestnut brown, green, yellow, pure white, or purple. What appeared to be a strange, pink ball in the middle of a rug of alder leaves was a soft, fleshy, intricate coral fungus (*Clavaria formosa*). It took us quite a while to reach the beach. Suddenly the path became sandy, leading to an opening that sent sunlight flooding into the forest. With reverence, I passed through. Such a dramatic line where forest ended and beach began—or was the beach ending and the forest beginning?

Watching the breakers, I thought of loved ones who, due to age or disability, could never come here. Maria the opera singer, whom I'd known since we were fourteen, would strain her back and perhaps seize up. Gram was too old. She had come to Long Beach before the highway was paved. Sara Jane said she was glad to have someone with whom she could share the place. Sid, a massive grey and white dog, part Irish wolfhound, with big light brown eyes, barked louder than the west coast wind.

Tofino power outages were common; therefore, so were woodstoves. We had to burn tree parts. Hemlock was preferable to cedar, because it lasts longer as it burns, but cedar will burn even when damp. We got our firewood from clearcuts; it was normal for locals to access slash. We would spend hours chainsawing, gathering, and hauling firewood, finally loading it into the back of a pickup. Ravens would call from above as we worked. Clearcuts always left tons of wood behind, but nurse logs were seldom left intact. Nowadays I feel that we should leave everything alone, as biodegrading nutrients for the stripped soil, a nursing ground for alder and fireweed—a way to bring back a forest more quickly.

I walked Sid often, not because he was neglected but because I enjoyed his company. On our own, we explored behind the B&B. There was a rough trail to Browning Passage, locally called "the Inlet." Along this trail the shrubs and short, often dead trees (i.e., marginal forest) gave way to climax rainforest. As usual, I was struck by the beauty and lush richness. From time to time, Sid would stop and wait for me. Sometimes he bounded off again as soon as he saw me; other times he waited until I spoke to him or touched him.

It was hard going. At one point I had to lie flat under a nurse log to get beyond it, and as soon as the dog saw me in that position he insisted on washing my face. Reaching the inlet at last, if the tide was out, the almost-full moon might be rising. Mud flats stretched out to small forested islands without light or noise pollution. Far away were hazy clear-cut mountains, bald and scarred. But no nearer, yet. One day I scanned with binoculars. A flock of gulls fed near a flock of sandpipers, and a lone blue heron hunted for fish. Sid got restless, so I took him around the point and was surprised to spot a human: Sara Jane! By the time we finished our visit, the forest was quickly darkening, and this time Sid did not wait.

There was a great place to have lunch in town called Organic Matters. I would don my rain gear and cycle downtown to volunteer at the Friends' office and at the Rainforest Centre. When a family from the Shetland Islands walked in, they were as surprised as I had been to learn that, centuries ago, Scotland's west coast was covered with hyper-oceanic temperate rainforest, dominated by Scots pine, oak, ash, and ancient Atlantic hazel. Other days, I helped Zoë on the blue box round (pickup day for recyclables). Riding on the back of the truck for two hours was a hoot. It was also how I got to know every road in and around town. Afterwards, we got free tea and a snack at the Common Loaf Bake Shop, which was owned by Tofino Councillor Maureen Fraser. A quote on the wall there read:

I swear it to you
I swear it on my common woman's head
The common woman is as common
As a common loaf of bread...
and will rise.

Nowadays the place is run by her smiling son, Lee. Its Facebook page claims: "Tofino's original whole foods bake shop. We say, 'Life is short, eat dessert first!'"

There was a small action targeting a meeting of the Sustainable Development Steering Committee. Environmentalists had abandoned their membership in the SDSC in '91 after the government refused to defer logging until an agreement was made. Three of us from FOCS stood at the table's corners, silently displaying laminated posters of clearcuts, landslides, and ruined rivers. The words HALT FORESTRY MALPRACTICE or OH, CANADA! headlined each shot, followed by the place, date, and name of the company responsible for the damage.

The meeting was a classic case of government and extraction company representatives against tourism and preservation—many men against two women, in fact. I didn't completely understand the proceedings, of course. But I could see that Maureen Fraser had most of the fingers pointing at her. She seemed to be having to defend a decision made by council the night before, one which she hadn't been happy with. It wasn't strong enough for real protection, yet to the companies it was *too* extreme. Near meeting's end, it sounded precisely like the men were merely discussing various ways to destroy Clayoquot Sound. Meanwhile, clearcutting was continuing day after day.

Indeed, Mac Blo "accidentally" cut trees in a biodiversity corridor at Tofino Creek. This became province-wide news when a resident found the mistake and reported it. Some of the Friends went to the site to document the damage done. An occupation of the Ministry of Forests in Port Alberni was planned for the next day. For some long-forgotten reason, I did not go.

Maureen resigned from the SDSC as council rep. Around the same time, we learned of the death of Petra Kelly, author and founder of the German Green Party. She and her partner were found dead in their flat. I remembered hearing her speak in Vancouver when I was a teenager. She stood for "uncompromising nonviolence, radical ecology, indivisible human and civil rights, civility, social emancipation, justice, and solidarity with the weak."

A few days later, SDSC had its very last meeting and dissolved without strategy consensus. FOCS had a large presence at the meeting, once again holding up laminated posters of clearcuts. There was a new union rep at the table who, I noticed, was red in the face. He said angrily that loggers "don't give a shit about clearcuts," because "all our marriages are splitting up." Only the tourism rep and the Tofino rep talked about the concept of developing new, alternative job industries. And now it was all moot. I wrote to the minister of economics and small businesses. If logging in Clayoquot Sound were to continue at pace, Tofino would lose tourism dollars. The stunning scenery would become raw brown clearcuts like everywhere else. That's why logging companies in many places tended to agree with "scenic buffering." It kept them at peace with the tourism industry and hid the truth from the public.

Premier Mike Harcourt told a conference about a so-called misinformation campaign in Europe against BC's forest industry, and he announced his plans to visit there the following spring to set things straight. The World Wildlife Fund had released a video in Europe exposing this province's appalling logging practices; the video was banned in Canada, according to my journals, though I didn't make note of who did the banning. The fight was heating up. Greenpeace Germany wanted half of BC saved and a moratorium on the other half, or so we'd heard.

In the midst of it all, I had my first kayaking experience. I was grateful to be taken out by seasoned kayaker George Yearsley, who these days is an artist known as Feather George for his carvings of gorgeous cedar eagle feathers. I had briefly met him two years prior, stuffing envelopes at Western Canada Wilderness Committee (WCWC) in Vancouver. He turned out to be a strong paddler, whereas I found it hard work. Kayaks are long and we were fighting the current. George led me across Browning Passage over to Wanačis-Hiłthuuʔis. We took a brief rest on a grassy tuft of land, where ducks, herons, and sleek black cormorants flew away from us. Then we headed straight for so-called Meares Creek. We left our kayaks on the mud and walked up the creek bed into the rainforest. I got to see what I'd been hearing about: spawning salmon. The huge fish all but clogged the shallow stream. Most of them were stranded in pools, prevented from travelling any farther by rocks, branches, logs, or extremely shallow waters. After several days of rain, the last thirty-six hours had been dry, causing a drastic fall in water level, and leaving the salmon trapped.

The trail kept us beside the creek. We went slowly, careful not to frighten the fish. It was tempting to help them on their way upstream, but George was against human interference in natural processes, and I decided to respect my guide's opinion.

We came upon a sudden open area. Here was a beautiful, tangled ground-sea of ferns and salal. There was no other colour or any barrenness to break the mosaic. Yet it felt the opposite of crowded. It was the rainforest's version of a meadow: a break in a landscape of trees, allowing ground-level plant life to stretch up into the humid air. I had hardly finished a quick intake of breath when my gaze was drawn to the northeast edge of this meadow, where an ancient Sitka spruce stood in silent dignity. I'd never seen anything greener. Coral fungi were abundant around the base of its trunk.

On the way out, we found a freshly killed headless fish lying on the bank, trickles of blood coming out of claw-puncture marks on its side. We assumed a bear had been either startled into leaving its meal, or else was not very hungry.

Back at our kayaks, we saw that the tide had drastically receded, so we had to move fast. George was obliged to pull me out of the mud more than once, and to show me how to push off with my paddle. The paddle wanted to sink into the mud. I was scared. Luckily, we made it to deeper water. The experience was worth the sore muscles. The following year, the trailhead was obliterated by blowdown during a storm.

November brought hours in a Victoria courtroom. A spirited, colourful, musical demonstration in front of the courthouse warmed us up for the trial of arrestees Sile Simpson and Dan Lewis. As the Tank was being sworn in to testify, he kissed the Bible. The prosecution lawyer talked for ages, even though both Sile and Dan were pleading guilty to contempt of court. Defence took only a brief turn afterwards. Mac Blo's lawyer pushed for harsh sentences of immediate jail time of thirty days for Sile and sixty for Dan. Sile's lawyer, Tim, was a kind, thoughtful man. I didn't understand why he wouldn't spend as long speaking to the judge. Why not take the time to meticulously address every statement MB's lawyer made? To our relief, the judge gave Sile a $1,500 fine suspended for twelve months, and gave Dan a $3,000 fine suspended for eighteen months. The story made the front page of the *Times Colonist*.

As trials continued, many blockaders "spoke to sentencing." This was a defendant's chance to explain her or his motive for blockading. It was a welcome break from legal-speak. Many of us shed tears as the speeches struck emotional chords and inspired us all to keep up the fight. Several arrestees agreed to a plea bargain and then pleaded guilty. Lawyers said pleading not guilty would only result in worse sentences.

Some people were being charged with civil contempt of court, like those who'd been arrested within the first few days of the blockade. They would most likely receive fines. I was one of those. We were charged for disobeying the court-ordered injunction not to interfere with Mac Blo's access to the forest. Others were being charged with criminal contempt. Civil contempt is elevated to criminal contempt if disobeying the court order is "public and/or flagrant." After the first arrests, the judge assumed everyone knew they would be arrested (flagrant), and knew there would likely be media (making the contempt more public).

Those arrested later were charged with criminal contempt under the civil code, not under the criminal code. The difference is significant, as criminal contempt can result in a sentence lasting up to two years, but does not provide defendants the same access to defence arguments accorded to criminal trials. Criminal contempt of court is a "grey area of the law." To add insult to injury, Mac Blo was suing for lost wages and reduced timber sales.

Friend and fellow arrestee Eric said calmly to the elderly judge, "Sometimes the state fails to provide just laws. I would ask you, My Lord, to think of your grandchildren." Under cross-examination he was steady and sensible. When asked if he had ever considered acting in certain legal ways to further his concerns about the forests, Eric listed a range of activities he had exhausted before resorting to blockading. I hadn't known our speeches could be cross-examined.

Afterwards, the judge requested Eric's lawyer's opinion on how to solve the problem (the logging, the jobs, the citizens' actions). I cheered inside: "The discussion becomes relevant at last!" Up until then, there was virtually no reference made by lawyers or judge to the reasons why people had broken the law in the first place. Instead, the focus was on proving that individuals were indeed on the road, preventing loggers from going to work. I saw, however, that the judge was not truly interested in what the lawyer had to say.

Painter Jim, Divina's dad, took the stand in his vest covered in buttons that said many of the same things our placards did. He called himself an aging hippie and spoke eloquently without notes.

Then Jean, the Raging Granny who was arrested as Mother Earth, took the stand. She was the first to point out to the judge that our actions were about saving jobs that machines were taking away.

Naming clear-cut logging and destruction, Jean looked the old man in the eye and said, "It is our generation who let this happen."

As she left the podium and walked back to her seat in the crowded benches, all of us stood up in her honour, retaking our seats only after she had taken her own.

On my twenty-fifth birthday a young protector was cross-examined in a gruelling manner after speaking to sentencing. A person's right to speak was clearly just another tool to be used against us. The lawyer made several objections, to no avail.

We had a calming circle before the sentencing of this batch, around the big oak in a nearby churchyard. Jan Bate led a grounding meditation and we sang songs. A kiss was passed around the circle. Everyone ended up hugging the oak and each other. But back inside the courtroom, the sentencing was worse than all six lawyers thought. Twenty days in prison. For first-time offenders! One of them was just getting to grips with a deep personal loss. Another was only twenty years old.

It was a horrible moment. The benches were still. We all sat in shocked silence. Then Tim, the lawyer, jumped up and asked the judge for the option of electronic monitoring anklets. Time served at home. The application would take three weeks to process; our people would be free during that time. The judge agreed. I seem to remember only one of the arrestees having a telephone in their home. Telus would soon have new Tofino customers. One couldn't serve time via electronic monitoring without a phone, or what we call a land line today. No one carried mobile phones back then.

My trial was coming in late January, and I was mentally preparing for a similar fate. My lawyer had pressured me to accept the plea bargain, but I was glad I hadn't. Obviously, it didn't do anybody any good! I resented being pressured. Out of principle I would plead not guilty. What I did was about clearcutting and the rainforest, not contempt for the court. I was glad to get other lawyers' opinions, because my own was not a fighter, knowing it was often no use. Nevertheless, I still valued her opinions, because she was familiar with most of the judges, and she knew I could get an even harsher judge in January.

A certain cop finally caught up with me at the courthouse, to talk about our complaints regarding police brutality. He wanted to interview me, but my lawyer got him to write his questions on paper. She'd later fax my answers to him. She didn't understand why I was so evasive until I privately explained that he was believed to be the head of a "political dissident investigation squad." In other words, he was keeping files on activists. I wasn't going to help him add to mine.

In December, something wonderful happened. Even the knowledge of definite jail sentences didn't scare Earth's protectors, and the cold winter darkness could not put them off: once again there were blockades every morning. Three men were arrested (one in his thirties, two in their fifties).

So much for interim freedom; two friends did go to jail for the weekend before being fitted with electronic anklets. They phoned and described it as smoky with terrible food. We phoned Norleen, who was in the city lock-up, since there was no women's facility on Vancouver Island. City lock-up was mostly full of drunk drivers and a few sex workers. The food came from A&W restaurants. Limp salad and greasy fries for lunch and dinner were the vegetarians' lot.

Therefore, it was not without a tinge of guilt that we took a day to go canoeing. Sara Jane came with us in her kayak. Sid was patient, but he was tempted by ducks flying by, to the point where he'd leap up and nearly flip the canoe. We had to speak in fierce tones to get him to lie down.

Then all was stillness and peace again except for a passing kingfisher with its chattering call and darting flight. We paddled close alongside one of the islands; it had no beach, only vertical rainforest, rock, and sea. After countless herons and cormorants, a pair of bald eagles flew low over our heads. Orange sea stars glowed in clear shallow water, and a squirrel chattered from boughs above. Around a corner, a seal with a mournful face lay on a rock. It cautiously slipped into the water. These were some of the creatures for whom our friends sat in prison.

By December 10, the "criminals" were back, anklets fitted, black boxes with flashing lights hooked up to telephones. It would only be a week, after all. They had scheduled time to go to work, but apart from those hours, they could not step beyond the doors of their homes. On the Monday, a young woman was arrested for blockading.

I was given a photo of Green and me at Schooner Cove / Esowista, with Sid jumping for a stick in mid-air. We stood in the centre of the beach; snowy mountains filled the horizon, with a forest-covered peninsula in the closer background. I'd been used to looking at that scenery for months, and was used to seeing my partner in it, but the photo was the first time I saw myself in it. It was home. And yet any joy was tinged, because the rainforest was more threatened than ever and I might not have written a letter in two weeks. In an apparently otherwise lifeless galaxy, our living planet was being scalped of its life support system.

I remember the day of that photograph. The waves were high, the clouds raced across the sky, and an eagle rode the wind, a branch in its talons. It was perfect viewing, with or without binoculars, for a long time. Only once did the talons lose their grip, drop the branch, and catch it again in mid-air. Even the dog watched. Finally, the bird released the branch and soared out to sea.

PUNISHMENT

Green and I cut firewood together on an invigorating, windy morning. Then he left for Garth Lenz's trial in Nanaimo. Garth was one of December's arrestees, and, like Valerie, he was on the FOCS board of directors at the time. He was "a tall, lanky, witty classical pianist who taught at the Royal Conservatory of Music and was to become one of Canada's premier photographers documenting forests and the tragedy of clearcutting," as Valerie describes him. He would go on to win several prestigious international photography awards. But for now, he would be defending himself.

I was sorry to miss his trial, but I lived in a dog's world. To qualify for house arrest we all needed homes, jobs, and telephones; my job would be dog-sitting. I was already taking care of one recent arrestee's dog. Dingo was a nervous creature, having been a stray. She stayed outside all the time, waiting for someone to take her for a walk. At night we had to catch her and carry her in. She and Sid got on extremely well, though he was jealous; they rubbed shoulders and scent-marked the same tufts of grass on the beach. Often their paths drifted apart; realizing this had happened, each suddenly stopped and stared across the sand at the other.

At the inlet one day, the tide was so high that the water lapped at the forest, and so I was at last obliged to really explore the trail. In doing so the dogs and I came across huge twisted old cedars. Nature was so inexplicable, so unpredictable. We ended up behind a tiny floathouse recently deposited on the rocks by wind. I was standing on the path, looking up at the noisy crows and jays, when I spotted a bird of prey sitting on the very top of a tall hemlock. Through binoculars it looked both fluffy and like a hawk. It peered around a lot, rotating its head but not moving its body.

The news came from Nanaimo that the judge would not allow Garth to use the legal argument of "defence by necessity"—i.e., when a person breaks the law to prevent something worse from happening, like breaking down someone's door to save a person from a burning building, but in this case interfering with clearcutting to prevent the planet from burning. But Garth got to talk a lot anyway. The judge seemed potentially sympathetic. Years afterward, friends would remind Garth of the phrase he used to petition the judge not to give him a large fine: "M'Lord, I don't have much incoming income coming in." Dingo's human had pleaded guilty and would not apply for home arrest if jail were sentenced. The other man and the young woman were contesting the label of criminal. Ultimately all four protectors were found guilty of criminal contempt. The one who pleaded guilty was fined $500; the others were fined $750.

There was another court date to attend, this time in Tofino. A bear protectors' hearing (to set a trial date) took place in the basement of the local Legion. The hearing concerned six people who interfered with a black bear trophy hunt the previous spring. At first, though, there was yet other court business to attend to. As many individuals accused of petty crimes were called forward, it became clear that only a few had bothered to turn up. Was this typical of small towns? Or was it typical of Tofino in particular? I didn't know, but the room was anything but empty. It was full of bemused bear protectors and their supporters. A well-known character called Turtle, who had been banned via actual town bylaw from laughing after 10:00 p.m., started his loud cackling. A police officer got up and made as if to go after him, and Turtle made as if to run for it. It was all for show. I think even the judge enjoyed it.

After the entertainment, a date for the bear trial was set, and we all flocked to Organic Matters where several people met with a probation officer. There were forms to fill in and community hours to arrange for convicted blockaders.

⁂

Never a dull moment! The American organization Ecotrust put a quarter-page ad in the *New York Times* telling the story of BC's rainforests and clearcutting, with particular references to Clayoquot Sound. The ad made headlines on television and in the papers. No doubt the government and the companies with all their millions would do countercampaigns, but at least they were the ones scrambling to respond this time.

Just before my trial, possession of bear gallbladders was banned provincially. Norleen gave me a "shield of protection" she'd made from beads and felt. I also had a new lawyer.

For the duration of the trial, sympathizers offered a safe space to all of us due in court. An apartment near the courthouse, it was a welcoming place to eat lunch and rest. Food was donated from various sources, and Grumpy Ann's cooking fed us all, supporters included. I never saw Ann in a grumpy mood. Her kindness and support were deeply appreciated. Her daughter Dana was sixteen when she was arrested in Kaxi:ks, during the summer of 1991.

Sitting in court was draining. Although it described the following year's proceedings, *Clayoquot Mass Trials: Defending the Rainforest* edited by Ron MacIsaac and Anne Champagne, could have easily been talking about ours: "Many felt the trauma of the trial was a worse punishment than the jailings that followed. The courtroom for them was a stressful steampot, a windowless room, a straitjacket of evidence with rules that stopped their defence efforts in their tracks." Once, to keep sane, I sat in the back row giggling with two girlfriends. Four people, Noah and the woman with whom I shared a police car, got twenty days' incarceration. If eligible for electronic monitoring, they might be lucky and get only one night in city jail, followed by one at the Nanaimo Correctional Centre (NCC), and then twelve days at home on electronic monitoring. I say "they," but I should say "we." The precedent was set for me to get the same punishment.

Jesse, a very young man sentenced the day before, was from Ontario, so he was not eligible for electronic monitoring. If I had only known, we could have arranged for him to stay with us. He was taken directly to jail. I was furious at his lawyer. As the judge left the courtroom and Jesse was being led away, the crowd roared "Shame!" Everyone went outside and hung around in the cold, waiting for the van to emerge so we could wave to Jesse, but the sheriffs knew we were there. They used another exit. Why were the courts coming to the aid of an extraction company, anyway? How was it helpful to not allow a prisoner to see his supporters waving goodbye?

That evening we went to the university to see the slide show that Garth and Valerie were taking to Europe. In a little more than a week they had raised more than $6,000, pretty good for back then. The slides showed west coast Vancouver Island rainforests and northern BC, Albertan and Saskatchewan boreal forests, as well as a Native Elders' blockade in northern Saskatchewan. The Elders called themselves Protectors of Mother Earth. They stood against the clearcutting of their homeland. Before bed as usual I worked on my speech-to-sentencing, and made notes I wanted my lawyer to mention in her final submission.

Our judge, Mary Saunders, was a serious, respectable, soft-spoken person. On some days, both sheriffs were women, while the usually female position of clerk reporter was filled by a man. Crown prosecutor Brian Rendell took the entire day to cross-examine Mick, proclaimed star employee of Seattle's Subway sandwiches, wearer of ponchos and berets, defender of himself. It was absolutely tedious. How excruciating trying not to laugh while being forced to watch, over and over again, the video of him singing "Another one bites the dust" during an arrest. Rendell also kept repeating a clip that showed Mick sitting with a dog on the logging road, the two of them howling together. Why? Nearly everyone in the courtroom burst out laughing when Mick called himself to the witness stand, causing both Rendell and the judge to do double takes.

In the stand, Mick created further mirth by telling the judge unnecessary, personal details about his love life. "I came to Canada in pursuit of a young woman named Lisa, Your Honour" (he always said "Your Honour" instead of the correct phrase, "My Lady"). "But later, our relationship wasn't going so well and I fell in love with another woman I met at the blockades." I think his point was to prove he was on the road not to block logging, but for love. A rumour was going around that when the woman he fancied cut off her long hair, he wrote her a twenty-page letter chastising her for doing so.

Our day of judgment was Friday, January 29, 1993.

Mick gave his final argument, which took a long time, followed by my lawyer giving hers. Then Rendell delivered his final argument against the three of us. (My friend Bill had been using the same lawyer I had.) We were the final three defenders from the summer, and the only ones to have pleaded not guilty.

Over lunch, Saunders wrote up her decision. She found us all guilty of criminal contempt, sentencing us to two years' probation and twenty days' incarceration. Mick, being American, was not eligible for electronic monitoring, so he had to go to jail. His sentence was not cut in half, as some had been by a previous judge. I actually felt sorry for him. He had been dead serious throughout the trial, yet we had laughed at him. Mind you, he was sexist and tried to make others look bad so that he might look more responsible in Saunders's eyes. He often repeated that he had not gone limp, which could only make me look worse for doing so, Gandhian method or not. More muscle-work for cops.

I forced myself to get up and read.

> My Lady:
> My forbears came from northern England and my background is working class. My great-uncle, William Wilks, was logging selectively on Mayne Island decades ago. All his life he was against clear-cut logging.

While living in England, I became involved with the British Trust for Conservation Volunteers, an organization that sends volunteers all over the UK doing practical conservation work. At the same time I was aware that our planet's last fragment of coastal temperate rainforest was disappearing, and that much of it happened to be on Vancouver Island.

Last June I completed a year's college course in England, achieving a Certificate in Land Use and Countryside Related Studies. This involved more practical work with a variety of ecosystems, habitat "management" and land use theory. I got to know the various conservation organizations, societies and government bodies in that country.

I find it amazing that people there are working so hard to preserve fragments of woods and patches of grassland, while we in Canada are working so hard to liquidate this magnificent work of nature, the intricate, delicate ecosystem of the temperate rainforest.

And now British groups are helping to save Clayoquot Sound and other areas in BC. They recognize the global importance of our rainforests, while our own government will not.

I have been writing to politicians since early high school. When at age fifteen I delivered my eight-page petition against cruise missile testing to my local MP and the testing went ahead anyway, I did not give up lobbying. For years I have attended political meetings, tried to keep myself informed and educated, attended legal demonstrations, volunteered for many groups including the Western Canada Wilderness Committee, visited the Carmanah and Walbran valleys, and written more letters.

In these letters I have stressed that our problem is the companies—their mechanization, their greed—not the loggers themselves, and that while we negotiate and continue to log at the same time, committees should be setting up alternative job markets for workers. For even if our precious jewels are not saved, at the rate of current cutting these men will be out of work in a few years. I gave up writing about reasons to save trees. Now my letters are taken up with how to save jobs. Still, massive clearcutting continues.

I have been in an untouched, exquisitely beautiful valley one summer and returned the next to find it invaded, cleared out, flattened. Road building requires blowing up an area with explosives. The term "harvesting" can be applied to crops on a farm, or possibly to a tree plantation, but not a rainforest.

Experiencing this, what took thousands of years to evolve and only months to erase, made me realize that my legal actions were not being taken seriously. I had also heard that it was blockading in the Walbran that resulted in deferrals on logging there.

So I joined the blockade in Clayoquot Sound.

I wish this trial could have been held in a clearcut or in the rainforests of Meares Island, and I would beg Your Ladyship, if you have not already, to go and spend some time in both settings yourself.

To end, I will just say that the reason I pleaded "not guilty" to criminal contempt might not make legal sense but it is my truth: I bear this court no contempt, and I am a protector, not a criminal.

Thank you.

I would write it differently today. I wouldn't use the possessive; they are not our forests, our jewels. I would use Tlaoquiaht place names and speak of unceded territories. I might call myself a concerned citizen. I would share what I learned from an Indigenous woman, that by learning the history of this place and its people, we correct colonial narratives like "wilderness."

As for Bill, a gentle, modest person, he didn't want electronic monitoring. "Let them pay for my time," he said. He spoke to sentencing simply by standing up and stating that he was proud of what he had done. I was glad he told the judge what no one else had dared tell her.

Now I was free until February 19. I phoned the electronic monitoring (EM) assessor at NCC. He was distinctly casual, so I stopped worrying about it. Sometimes I felt like I almost wouldn't mind doing the jail time, but it would have had to be kept secret from my Gram, and I wouldn't have wanted Green bothering himself with constant visits. Mind you, I'd probably feel different once I was inside! A friend and I visited Jesse at Wilkinson Correctional Centre. All the tables and chairs were locked to the floor, and the vast majority of visited inmates were young with long hair. Ours was doing okay. It was his last night of incarceration.

In February when I phoned the EM assessor again, he asked a lot of questions. In the end, he said he would recommend me for the house-arrest program. Whew! I wouldn't even have to sleep in city lock-up. The judge agreed to allow my sentence to start on the same day as those who pleaded guilty started theirs.

The whole court appointment was very brief, maybe ten minutes.

Crown counsel was a friendly pregnant woman who made no objections. I had the flu, so was doubly relieved. Imagine eating jail food and breathing cigarette fumes while sick. When the others were appearing before their judge, Tim requested that they be allowed to make their own way to NCC very early the next morning, so that their processing could happen the same day, and not a single night need be spent in Victoria lock-up or NCC.

Then it was my turn. I was used to the formal, sombre brow of Justice Saunders, who kept to the bowing routine, speaking softly and formally, with great seriousness if not sternness. In contrast, out swaggered a judge who literally threw himself into his chair without bowing. Gesticulating wildly, he started laughing to Tim about a mix-up between himself and a judge with a similar name. Meanwhile, Tim humoured his lordship as best he could. Then suddenly the old man leaped up and walked out with a final laugh! I had no idea what had taken place until someone told me: the judge had agreed to Tim's request.

Our processing at the prison in Nanaimo went from about 9:00 a.m. till just after 1:00 p.m. (I stopped calling it a "correctional centre.") There were four of us being fitted, and two friends were allowed in with us (one being Green, my partner). I was taken upstairs by myself so someone could write my description down and take my picture. While I waited, an inmate offered me coffee, and a young man was handcuffed and escorted out. I don't remember any other women being there. I do remember a poster above someone's desk, of Garfield the cat exclaiming: "Well, DUH!" Damn giggle reflex!

I found a lot of things funny. The ludicrous situation, for a start. Concerned people punished for trying to save a forest. Truth be told, we all had a lot of laughs in the EM office. It was discovered that I hadn't signed my probation order. I *had* had a sneaking suspicion that there was something I ought to have done, but how was I to know the ins and outs of incarceration? It had slipped by the sheriffs, never mind me. Therefore, I was driven to the courthouse where the form was faxed from Victoria. We went through the dungeon (Nanaimo city lock-up), which was horrid, worse than the prison: dark cells, sounds of men shouting somewhere deep within, and the feeling of being watched.

Back in jail, we all waited around while our curfew schedules were being programmed on the computer. Richard, the man in charge of electronic monitoring, was doing mine.

"Why doesn't anyone work nine to five anymore?" he grumbled, punching keys.

"Too much stress?" I suggested. He gave me a look that could kill.

The nice older man, Alan, fitted us with our ankle bracelets. He was laughing with us. A certain woman was the first. She pulled up her pant leg to reveal thick, dark shin hair. Alan didn't flinch.

Maybe Richard resented not being in on the laughs; maybe he felt his power was undermined, or that we weren't taking our doom seriously. At one point he growled something about putting my shackle around my neck. Finally he called everyone into a room to read us some rules under the heading "Temporary Admitted Absence from NCC." We filed in, and one of us sat down.

"Don't sit down!" he shouted angrily. "Stand up!"

Out of my mouth came, "This guy's got bad karma." I wished I hadn't said it. After his tantrum, I started to fold my paper. "Don't fold it!" he shouted. I almost laughed. For a moment I struggled with the corners of my mouth, but he wasn't looking.

Surprisingly, we were allowed to make our own way to Tofino without an escort. When I got home, I bathed, and the prison had trouble with my signals after that. They phoned me in the middle of the night a couple of times, but apparently this was normal practice. The box and strap were so loose on my ankle, I could have easily slipped free.

During one of the calls, I was told I could have two free hours on both days of the weekend. Meanwhile I was outdoors for most of my shifts, doing the blue box recycle run and taking Jazmin to

Tonquin Beach. Jazmin was a large, long-haired rascal of a dog. Every day she moped around Organic Matters, but at the beach she transformed into a clever trickster—affectionate and playful, until her eyes turned psycho and she charged like a bear. Then she'd veer off and push her face into the shallow creek streaming over the sand.

A few days later Alan came all the way to Tofino to fit me with a new unit, because mine wasn't working. In fact, since that first bath I could have come and gone freely without them knowing. The unit was worth thousands of dollars and was supposed to be entirely waterproof.

Meanwhile, Premier Harcourt asked the public to phone him with their wishes on the fate of Clayoquot Sound. Two Friends directors were interviewed on the CBC nine o'clock news. On March 5, we forest defenders were allowed to unplug ourselves, pack up our units, and take them to Tofino's police station, where a cop clipped the straps and set our ankles free. Since it was a day early, we had to be good little environmentalists and stick to an 11:00 p.m. curfew that night. It had been twelve days.

Rain gear on, the next day I took Sid and Mistaya (yet another dog, from yet another arrestee) to Tin Wis beach. Because the tide was so low, the waves came in from opposite directions around a rock islet. They met in a line like a frothing seam being sewn. The foghorn was sounding. I'd heard an anecdote about a visitor who thought the echoing tones were whales making love. He subsequently raved about the wild romance of this place, or so the story goes, and went home saying everyone should come here during grey whale mating season.

DECISION FALLS WITH A C.L.U.D.

It was around this time that Green and I began to stick our noses into town issues. Put another way, we chose to get involved with the place we now called home. The Wickaninnish hotel hadn't been built yet and Chesterman Beach was considered the last beach for locals, while other stretches of sand were thought to have already been taken over by tourists. Oh, the arrogance of white folk, making a fuss at the threat of losing "our" last beach.

A community meeting took place, or was it a public hearing? The council chamber was too small for such a gathering; people were crammed into the doorways and standing outside. Three young men showed drawings, aerial photos and models of the proposed hotel. A question period was followed by time for more general comments. I had been standing at the back for ages when a friend spoke up and joked that she was a member of FOWL: Friends of What's Left. I don't remember what else she said. Then I took a turn, raising my concern at the inevitable traffic increase, and mentioning how my roommate's dog was killed by a car in the autumn. To my surprise, some people scoffed and laughed. Why so many rooms, I stammered on, when it might be empty all winter? We all know about the problem of homelessness in Tofino (these days it's province-wide and called the Housing Issue). Then I dropped what turned out to be a bomb: visitors at that kind of a swanky hotel would be looking for luxury and might not respect a place like this.

Outcry! from those who had scoffed at my roommate's dog.

A man then claimed to be among the "first here forty years ago," and it was a good thing he wasn't so particular about who joined the community, or a lot of us wouldn't be here!

In any case, we had other worries, like the fact that the BC government was expected to make their decision any day as to how much of Clayoquot Sound would remain open to logging. Concerned citizens were keeping a constant vigil on the legislature lawn in Victoria, and finally Harcourt agreed to meet with WCWC soon. I didn't record in my journal whether any other groups were invited to the meeting. Whatever resolution came down, it would tell us how much we still had to fight for. The Sound was now being promoted as BC's Hawaii since tourism might save it from logging.

> For every person willing to risk arrest, there were thousands more who were angry and worried sick about the carte blanche logging companies were given to "manage"—by clearcutting—primary rainforests. These companies were allowed to take trees hundreds of years old, destroy animal habitats, and cause terrible landslides that deposited dirt and debris into precious salmon streams and rivers. During the Rio Earth Summit in June 1992, governments world-over committed to turn the tide on precipitous loss of biodiversity. Yet, back at home those same governments approved logging that could only be described as a devastation approach. People were fed up with … empty promises to address the global crisis alongside laws that exacerbated it and then criminalized the people who stood peacefully to stop the destruction.
>
> —Valerie Langer

On our way down to a rally in Victoria, we heard news reports that a crowd had stormed the legislative assembly and nearly got inside the actual chamber, breaking an old stained glass window and accidentally hurting a guard. Jean McLaren was there and described what she saw in the introduction to *Spirits Rising*. Much later, I watched the TV news footage; I saw that the instant the guard went down, a young person was offering him help. What did not make the news was the fact that money was collected afterwards to pay for the window, and an apology card full of signatures sent to the guard. Sound like rioters to you?

At its peak, the crowd was said to have reached five hundred. By the time we got there no one was inside anymore. People were on the steps and grass, and there was a little bit of laid-back drumming and dancing. Soon a microphone was set up under a tarp and an Indigenous woman spoke, bringing tears to my eyes. Environment Minister John Cashore came on and made the mistake of scolding the crowd for the earlier "violence." He was booed. Gordon Wilson, BC Liberal leader, spewed his own dogma. There was an unsavoury incident when WCWC's Paul George tried to silence a woman by intimidating her with his body, moving threateningly toward her. The TV cameras zoomed in on them until a small senior stepped smoothly in front of everyone with a sign that said something about saving Clayoquot. It was Ruth Masters. I hoped she had her harmonica and serving spoons nearby.

After a slew of speakers, a woman named Adriane Carr from WCWC spoke. She was nearly overcome with emotion and passion. I admit, I was caught. (She is Paul George's wife!) Then Dana got to say something in defence of what happened inside. She was cheered.

The next day the *Province* (with the dramatic headline "RIOT" over a picture showing half a dozen people calmly walking up some stairs), the *Times Colonist* and the *Vancouver Sun* gave the story their front pages, and it was the *Globe and Mail*'s first "news brief" on its front page. The last line in one of the *Province*'s opinion pieces was: "If I was Mr. Harcourt I would pave the Clayoquot."

Well! Any coverage was good coverage.

WCWC made an apology and a statement denying all responsibility for the "riot" (they organized the rally). The incident was apparently an abuse of the democratic process. Au contraire! It was people taking charge, using that process to its fullest. They wanted to get face to face with those who were elected to represent us—and talk. Why was the legislative assembly closed? This was not the as-yet unimaginable 2021 White House riot south of the border. These kids were not about to start beating up MLAs. No one carried weapons. Politicians afraid to face citizens deeply affected by their decisions are cowards in my view. It was our future they were discussing in there.

There came word of charges being pressed against those who had "stormed" the legislature. There were also rumours that some of them were infiltrators, planted to make environmentalists look bad.

Later I found out that my Gram had telephoned various politicians whilst I was incarcerated, and told them what a disgrace it was to jail people for trying to stop clearcutting. "My granddaughter is SHACKLED!" she told them, again and again.

Immediately upon returning to Tofino, we rushed off to a council meeting. Some councillors wanted to change a resolution made months previously regarding Tofino's stance on government-proposed land use plans for Clayoquot Sound. These members wanted to inform the provincial government that Tofino now agreed with "option five" (which apparently called for cutting 88 percent of the Sound). Discussion grew intense as two other councillors fought it all the way; after all, the decision already made was supposed to have been final. Regardless, an amended or slightly altered letter was passed and we had to assume that the government, the companies, and Share groups would pounce on it, using it as an excuse to continue and expand logging. The amendment was based on a supposed 150 residents who, although they did not attend community meetings, were against the original decision and had lobbied a single councillor to make the change on their behalf. They claimed she was elected thanks to them.

At the meeting, I found myself thinking of both past and future. I had been reading about Tofino's settler history. One book in particular called *Lone Cone* by Dorothy Abraham (first published in 1945) had struck me with its total optimism. Dorothy was a war bride who left her beloved England to live with her husband on Vargas Island, Clayoquot Sound. Describing her vision for Canada, she wrote about what a wonderful country it would be when it was all roaded and mined, "with all its resources put to their fullest use." Yet I knew that if Mrs. Abraham could have been in that council room, she would have been horrified. She wrote, immediately following the above quote, "But come what may it is lovely to think that nothing can ever destroy the wonderful rugged beauty of this coast." I hoped she had passed on before she could see how wrong she was.

At the same time, I was imagining future residents and visitors shaking their heads and saying to one another, "What a tragedy it was allowed to happen." Then I thought of how the forest's inhabitants were, at that very moment, having death sentences passed over them by oblivious council members. But no, they were not oblivious.

One particular councillor kept contradicting himself, going from one side to the other. His boat burned later that night. There was no evidence of foul play, yet the *Province* said FOCS did it! The paper neglected to mention the fact that his son was having a party on board at the time. Maybe someone would sue that press for libel, joining the list of Tofino's lawsuits. Someone was suing council for misrepresentation. Many of us had our names on a lawsuit against the hotel developers. And then there were the Mac Blo and Fletcher Challenge SLAPP suits—Strategic Lawsuits Against Public Participation. These suits were used by industry and government to attempt to intimidate citizens with legitimate grievances into silence. Meanwhile an elderly activist's tires were slashed on another night. Why didn't the media report it?

When the meeting was over, a Channel 6 BCTV cameraman interviewed several residents. It was a strange thing to live at the hub of national news. The very next day we turned on the radio only to hear two Tofino councillors being interviewed on a national show. This was two days after CBC Radio's program *BC Almanac* focused on Clayoquot Sound, featuring interviews with many locals. Yet, at the same time, FOCS couldn't find another office as eviction time loomed. And all this attention wasn't stopping Interfor (International Forest Products, another multinational company clearcutting Clayoquot) from opening its own office in Tofino. MB, of course, remained the company with the most claim in Clayoquot.

Around this time, Harcourt's NDP government was revealed to have just purchased shares in Mac Blo. They were now the company's biggest shareholder! Gram wanted me to phone my MLA to ask why they bought the shares. She had supported the NDP since she was young (when it was the CCF), only to be thus betrayed in the twilight of her life. "Rarely has a government so consciously destroyed its traditional voting base," said a *Victoria Star* editorial.

We took a UK environmental photographer over to the Big Trees Trail. He took dozens of shots of the giants. We saw a jellied mass of frog eggs in a stream, and a new eagle nest on Morpheus Island. Later the photographer went "moonscaping" in a seaplane, photographing the miles and miles of clearcuts.

Journalists, filmmakers, videographers and writers were arriving from all over the world to gather visuals and information, spreading their images and words of the ugly truth far and wide.

There was so much change that spring, but as young people we took it in stride. We were about to move to a log cabin on Stockham Island (a five-minute motorboat ride from Tofino's docks), and I joined a travelling play. It was about an environmentalist and a logger caught in a forest fire, thus forced to work together or die. The publicity leaflet, written by Mac, our director, said: "Written using grassroots research methods, we will come to you for ideas. Exploring issues affecting us all on Vancouver Island, and using the methods of forum theatre, this production gives you a chance to get involved! *That Damn Stage Behind the Rad Collective Theatre Society* is a collective formed to produce community-based theatre of a political and/or educational nature." I would have preferred "topical," "controversial," or "activist" instead of "political." Still, not bad for someone in their early twenties. So many at our age were apathetic instead.

Some of us in the cast drove to Ucluelet to interview Mike Morton, director of Share BC. Share groups were connected to the Wise Use movement in the US: pro-industry, pro-clearcutting groups that tried to put forth an image of grassroots community support. But Share BC was funded by logging companies. Their placards said SHARE BC while our blockade placards said SHARE THE STUMPS.

Mac wanted to meet Morton to hear how a company employee might like himself portrayed. We all wanted our logger to be realistic and convincing, not a stereotype. Unfortunately, Morton never turned up. And there we were, four undesirables sitting in Smiley's café, real enemy territory. Kath's bright fuchsia hair and loud laugh, our unusual clothes, the men's long hair, not to mention a couple of nose rings—these were rare in Ukee back then. But nobody bothered us.

At the end of March, the "leader" of the European Economic Community said that BC's forestry practices were a model for the rest of the world. (Sure—of how not to log.)

By April, we had acquired an old motorboat and were doing the necessary cleaning and sanding. Whenever we were at work under the hull, Sid loved to trot over and wash our faces. Maybe he was looking for food in Green's almost-beard. In reasonable weather we would be able to paddle to town from the cabin—not be slaves to a motor. We quickly learned about variables like full moon tides. Low tide could signify potential danger where the route was otherwise quite safe; rocks might appear that were usually submerged, some with nasty sharp points. Or worse, they remained unseen just under the surface. Low tide is a smart time to go kayaking or canoeing, both for close-ups of tidal life and to scope safe routes.

We borrowed a friend's boat to begin moving possessions over to the cabin. As we traversed the water, my colonized mind thought of Emily Carr on her travels to Indigenous villages around BC. She'd be clutching her dog close to her, hanging on to her bags and whatever vehicle was transporting her. A lot of my valued possessions (books, tapes) sat in boxes near to water level on this tiny boat. The waves made by the motor sprayed onto them.

The cabin was visible from the inlet, though trees have grown up and hidden it since. We were fully aware that the home we were living in was made of trees. From the size of the logs, the trees were clearly second growth. We also saw bumper stickers in town that admonished readers to try wiping their butts with a spotted owl, the other threatened old-growth-dependent bird. There is no dignity or justification in producing toilet paper made from ancient rainforests broken down to pulp. There are toilet papers made from 100 percent post-consumer recycled paper. There are tree-free toilet papers. Our new composting toilet was soon set up in the wood shed. We added a bit of peat moss that came with it, and some soil. We would switch to sawdust for daily use, or seaweed, because peat moss is a non-renewable resource. It was a relief to spread ashes over the poop heap under the outdoor privy, which we would never use except to look for salamanders. To use the new one, you just stood on the step and seated yourself on the throne. We'd be turning the "drum" to help speed the composting process.

Our landlords had a private dock around the corner. I stood on the ramp there, looking down through the shallow green water. Under the surface were orange spiky urchins and a sunflower sea star with twenty-four arms. The star was a beautiful blend of colours, and seemed to me like something from outer space. Since sea star wasting disease began, I have seen common sea stars ("starfish") but never another sunflower star. Nothing with more than five arms yet.

On the trail from dock to cabin, we passed a well that would provide our drinking water. The forest welcomed us with several giant cedars. Both cabin doors were thick, heavy wood; I wondered what the builder had in mind, storms or bears. Probably both. Inside, all the windowsills were nice and wide, for plants and shells and feathers. Two large front windows showed the peaks of Hiłthuuʔis, with the sun rising above them or shining on them, or with the sunset turning them pink, just as beautiful as any postcard of tropically rainforested mountains. Hiłthuuʔis to this day remains covered with a year-round, thick, teeming, shaggy coat, although I cannot pretend to not have noticed recent thinning patches and browning due to long summer periods of no rain. The peaks look down on a wide expanse of water, which recedes at low tide to reveal the Arakun mud flats, every shorebird's buffet table. We could also see Neilson and Morpheus Islands from the front deck. The main room was for cooking, dining, and living. There were two tiny round sinks, side by side. The woodstove was nice and small, so it wouldn't "eat" too much wood. There was even dry firewood stacked in the shed ready for us to use. Entirely off the grid, the cabin offered no other heating or cooking source. We bought a miniature oven: an aluminum box to be placed on top of the hot woodstove. We baked an eggplant in it, and chocolate chip cookies. A rep for Energy Alternatives, Green would soon be setting up solar panels to power lights and radio. We had no TV or computer. What we did have was a radio phone. When we conversed on that, we'd have to say "over" and let go of a button so that the person at the other end could take their turn speaking.

Mounted via footstool, a tall double bed reached another window, where a view of the Arakun Islands would greet us every morning (except in thick fog). Behind the Arakuns, and beyond Wačis-Hiłthuuʔis, lurked a giant clearcut: the whole face of a mountain shaved, complete with roads and slides. It has since greened up, except for the roads and slides. Looking back, despite knowing the various sufferings life would bring, I marvel at our fortune, this cabin in Clayoquot for $300 a month.

It was so close to where Opitsat village was burned to the ground by an American trading captain in 1792. Some histories should be taught to everyone, as soon as we arrive. Sooner. We look around at unknowable time. The chaotic shapes of the trees, windblown and rain-lashed lichen clinging onto their broken and twisted branches. The islands' shorelines that shrink and grow with each tide, life covering every millimetre up to the forest's edge, where curving cedar boughs are hung with eelgrass, husmin (kelp) and colonies of barnacles. Off Tin Wis beach in 2005 that captain's descendants made public apology, and ƛaʔuukwiiʔatḥ Chiefs accepted.

The RCMP's verdict on my two complaints finally arrived in the mail; as had been expected, it declared a lack of enough evidence. Reading it, I had to laugh. Objecting about the cops to the cops. Mere formality. Now I could appeal to the Complaints Commission.

A form letter came to the Friends' post office box from a guy with big hopes and plans for restoring logged areas—something the government should have been paying people to do. I didn't, however, agree that hemp would restore clearcuts. Hemp requires a lot of nutrients from soil. I agreed that hemp is a versatile plant that should be farmed for paper and clothing, but not on the fragile ground that grew a temperate rainforest. Instead, native fireweed, salal, huckleberry and alder would naturally recolonize, bringing back nutrients.

In Vancouver, outside Mac Blo's annual general meeting a demonstration against SLAPP suits went well. Several riot cops stood around with nothing to do. There was good media coverage. A few short days later word came that the fate of Clayoquot Sound was finally going to be announced on April 13, 1993—and that Harcourt was coming to Tlaoquiat to make the statement. Three weeks after his government had become Mac Blo's largest shareholder!

Green and I went to the FOCS office first thing on the thirteenth, where we heard that the golf course was booked for the announcement and press conference. We got into a car with several others. Once we reached the golf course, we could hear helicopters landing farther south at the airport. Off we went again, only to stand around for ages in the cold and wet. U-TV news was there, as was a BCTV camera. The choppers that had landed were International Woodworkers of America (IWA), Share, or Mac Blo people, we weren't sure which. Possibly all of them. The passengers now stood around the machines, looking bored, like decoys. None of them seemed familiar.

We heard at that point that the Wickaninnish Centre had also been booked, but since a paddy wagon and several police cars suddenly appeared, we reckoned we already must be in the right spot. The Weigh West Hotel (currently Tofino Resort & Marina) was also booked, but was never used. Harcourt never had the guts to go into the village of Tofino.

Somebody soon wondered if the cops were here to blockade us, so it was decided to gradually trickle away toward the Wick. This plan was postponed when a large convoy of locals arrived. It seemed like the whole town was there. Catherine, an artist, brought her big wooden black-on-white banner: CLAYOQUOT SOUND: SAVE WHAT'S LEFT. The helicopters buzzed off again.

We knew Harcourt would land at the airport, because an ally listening to a hand held heard the pilot of the premier's private jet announcing its landing plans. The slick little plane finally landed, but it was a while before Harcourt came out to join his chosen few and hand-picked media. We were all still outside the runway wondering what was going on, the four choppers having returned.

I watched our premier and his cronies milling around the private plane for which taxpayers had paid. I saw the sleek, expensive machine and the rich men in their suits. I had tried to dress conservatively that morning. The world needs radical changes, so why feel silly or lose nerve about doing colourful actions? We all could have dressed up in animal costumes: eagles, bears, wolves, cougars, raccoons, otters, and marbled murrelets. Inhabitants who lose their homes to clearcutting. As Dan said, these animals don't have an escape condo in West Van. This is their only home.

Finally, the power clique got back into their machines and flew away again. As our long convoy began to drive frantically toward the golf course, someone in our vehicle who had heard a cop utter the words "Something suspicious is happening" decided she agreed with him. At that moment, a couple of vans drove by in the other direction. The BCTV cameraman appeared in one of the windows, gesturing madly at us to turn around and follow him. We screeched to a stop and did so, narrowly avoiding an accident.

We had just turned down the road to Wickaninnish when, for some reason, the convoy came to a halt. Dozens of confused people got out of their cars: activists, media, Share, and two Parks Canada employees. Some were swearing in anger, others were laughing at the wild goose chase. A government afraid of its people!

Suddenly a familiar little pickup whizzed by and Tina, a Tofino resident, popped her head out. "Radar Hill!" she yelled. The chase resumed. At the bottom of Naćaas we passed a cop car. At the top (in the miserable grey weather, which conveniently hid the clear-cuts from view), at last, was the premier, plus Environment Minister John Cashore and Forests Minister Dan Miller, huddling together around a microphone, facing the media. And now us. I later heard that this trip for Harcourt and his press cost taxpayers $30,000.

I recall local Sharon Whalen heckling Harcourt, who was just ending his speech. Clayoquot Sound would not go to the CORE (Commission on Resources and Environment) process, he said. That removed the talk portion from talk-and-log. Reporters kept referring to "the War in the Woods" in their questions. Organic Matters proprietor Fiona McCallum said in a loud, clear voice that everyone heard: "There is no *war*; we are not a violent people, we are a very peaceful people. Let that be clear."

"Who speaks for the bear and the salmon?" cried George, and I was reminded of my musings on animal costumes.

"I don't mind working," said a logger to Sharon.

"Nobody ever promised you a job for life," she replied. "Nobody ever promised me a job for life. I've changed my career." He didn't reply.

At first, I couldn't bring myself to look at the map that was on display. As usual, the companies won while both Earth protectors and the IWA were unhappy. A chunk of land had been added to Strathcona Park, but declaring a park ignores Indigenous land title. Besides, the newly protected bits were mostly bog or alpine rock, not dense rainforest, according to Valerie.

Ironically, the map was mostly green: the colour for Integrated Management (read clearcut logging). Most of the rest was coded for either "wildlife," "recreation" or (the biggest one) "scenic." This simply meant logging, with those things "in mind." I would like to point out that those three things should *always* be in mind, with any logging.

I was sure that every one of us had voted NDP in the previous election. Of course, any party might lose its backbone as soon as it is elected. How to disarm the multinationals? How to change the laws? Looking on the positive side, two watersheds were now saved, including the beautiful twenty-thousand hectare Megin. I went under house arrest for these places. It worked! And yet, as Valerie pointed out, what about the chilling reality when we considered there are ninety-one watersheds over 5,000 hectares on Vancouver Island and only six now remained intact? And only two of those were protected. The rest of the continent's situation was even worse.

Back in town, we caught the CBC six o'clock news. Harcourt's decision was the main headline, and the reports were both long and sympathetic, especially Ian Gill's (who detailed the cat-and-mousing). It also made the front-page headlines in all the papers. Other news: Paul Watson of Sea Shepherd announced he was forming a group to spike trees in Clayoquot that summer. According to Ecodefense, that had already been taken care of years before, in "thousands" of trees all over Wanačis-Hiłthuuʔis.

Later, after warming up, we went along to Wickaninnish School for the FOCS meeting. A big crowd materialized, including two TV news cameramen and Ian Gill. He was thanked for his excellent coverage. We all agreed: at least everyone watching the news had learned how anxious Harcourt was to avoid the people whose lives his decision would impact.

Items on the agenda were:

- what do we do now?
- meeting with First Nations
- making a map for a Wilderness Option
- what to tell callers (in the office) when they asked, "What can we do?"

The BC Ombudsman later confirmed that the government failed to consult First Nations about the April 13 decision on the Sound. I do hope that such an omission could never happen today.

It turned out that a lot more of the public were angry, and the media much more sympathetic, than I had expected. It was no use resentfully asking where they all were before the decision was passed. Before those shares were bought, before this decision was announced, Harcourt's government had been considered by some as the greenest BC had ever had. But he dug his heels in on Clayoquot, because logging companies were such a powerful economic force for the province. What would they do for fallers when they had cut down the last tree? Where was the eco in economy? The fact was, the contentious Clayoquot Land Use Decision (CLUD) may have been the best thing Harcourt could have done to help us fight clearcutting. It was something we hadn't had hanging over our previous blockades. A lot of people were phoning the office wanting to become FOCS members, and to become actively involved. Green reckoned there would be a major blockade soon. He was right.

The following day, from the cabin, I heard a blast. A horrible sound, shuddering through the air. Companies using explosives to make more roads. Sile Simpson told me she wanted to do a Walk to Ucluelet, and talk to loggers there. (She once walked around Northern Ireland, her homeland, with the message "Peace is possible.") I was thinking very hard about the potential of Mac's play. Our troupe would be setting out in early June.

Meanwhile, some of FOCS had been meeting with elected and hereditary Nuučaaňuł Chiefs. The Chiefs wanted a statement from the entire environmental community of Tofino. Sile and a few others took a banner and walked to Ucluelet, spending a night at the Esowista Reserve, Schooner Cove. The Ukee loggers weren't very friendly. But there was good coverage, including photos in the *Times Colonist* and the *Province*.

I started hoping for federal or UN intervention in Clayoquot Sound. Harcourt kept saying the CLUD was final, but with the continual and scathing media commentary, I didn't see how it could be. Harcourt had to have been losing sleep at night. The only thing that got as much media was war. In the *Vancouver Sun*, Stephen Hume wrote an angry response to the decision. He was Gram's hero. One paper showed that some areas in the "Scenic Corridor" had already been clear-cut right down to the water!

Meares Island, Wanačis-Hiłthuuʔis, was not included in the decision because it was still tied up in Land Claims court, despite being declared a Tribal Park in 1984 by its people. But all of Vancouver Island is Indigenous land. Most of British Columbia lies beyond the treaty frontier.

Three months after their hearing, the bear trials came. One woman and five men were charged with various offences from mischief and dangerous boat driving to theft—or was it possession of stolen property (a bear hide)? A year previously they had interfered with a bear shoot around Grice Bay, preventing more than one bear's death and placing the killed bear's hide in a cave held sacred for centuries by local First Nations.

The trial took place in downtown Tofino. As usual, it was standing room only. This was the first truly interesting trial I'd been to, with jokes thrown in by five chucklesome lawyers. There was even a good chance of winning. I was gobsmacked at the way the lawyers spoke to the judge. The submissiveness and respect displayed in Supreme Court during our trials were all but absent here. These guys knew they were the best in the province, addressing a small-town judge.

The man who held the trophy hunting licence for practically all of Vancouver Island was a sullen character. The young guide in his employ earned $150 a day plus $250 per kill. Before the new law was passed the previous February, these men were extracting bear gallbladders to sell to Asia. This fact was often brought up by defence lawyers to make them look worse, and it did. Our Bear Watch activists couldn't help holding the high ground next to such people. The prosecuting lawyer had some hard work on his hands.

The judge had big blue eyes and looked tired and fed up. He acquitted one man due to lack of evidence, and received roaring applause. At the end of all the evidence, he sighed, put down his papers and exclaimed: "Well!" Everyone burst out laughing, but the judge was serious. He said he wanted time to make his judgment, and he confessed that he used to be a hunter many years ago. We wouldn't hear his judgment until late the following month.

The BCTV cameraman was hovering around outside, interviewing the accused, lawyers, and supporters. The crowd was flanked by Ruth Masters's placards. This time her message was: PROUD TO DEFEND CLAYOQUOT'S BEARS.

I remember an evening's inspiring FOCS meeting with lots of new, mostly young faces. We learned that there was plenty of international reaction to the CLUD. Domestically, Canada's federal opposition party (Liberals) had officially supported total preservation. Svend Robinson (NDP member of Parliament) was willing to get arrested! This was what had happened to South Moresby of Haida Gwaii; it was going to be logged "until the Feds stepped in." Only now, the whole world wanted to step in. Harcourt was receiving letters from the Movement for a Green India, among others.

OF MAYPOLES AND MURRELETS

One afternoon, two juvenile and three adult bald eagles came together for a feast on the rocky beach just below our cabin. They were taking turns eating what appeared to be an octopus. They were around for so long that I had time to search for and find the video camera (which I had never used before). Its battery was dying but I managed to shoot, for several minutes, all five eagles huddling like a football team over their meal. They tugged with their beaks and pulled with their talons, but never got entirely out of the water. As more of it was consumed, room around it shrank. Eventually only one eagle could eat at a time. The others waited patiently, watching or preening, until another decided it had loitered long enough. It flew at the bird who was eating and took its place. I was surprised that there were no fights, not even one complaint. How confident the young ones were! Their elders treated them as equals. As one juvenile flew away, a new, third one appeared. Each bird had a unique pattern to its mottled wings.

Finally, only one juvenile and one mature bird were left. I crept out onto the deck. Now I could hear talons shifting, feathers shuffling. Then I noticed eagles all around me in the trees. It was impossible to know how aware of me they were, or whether I bothered them. In the same moment a flock of geese flew overhead, a loon made its lonely cry on the water, and a hummingbird whizzed past my face.

Maybe it was my presence, after all, that made the last two eagles leave. Later I clambered down there to investigate the cephalopod remains, but they were inaccessible under the surging tide. I gazed around at a calm sunset. Two seals watched me from the water.

I couldn't resist calling, "Hullooooo." A chattering kingfisher, two hummers, and the usual ducks and gulls were lively features of the land-and-seascape. It wasn't a quiet locale, but all the noise was wild. The last thing I saw before re-entering the trail was a vertical strip of rainbow up Lemmens Inlet, coming out of low clouds over Hiłthuuʔis.

In those days, rituals were a thing, like celebrating the equinoxes and solstices, thanks to Starhawk and Wicca workshops and Witch Camp. For many, these were lifelong practices; for me they faded away as many of our Wiccans left Tofino over the years. But soon after we moved to Stockham Island there was a continental event. People on Vancouver Island, the lower mainland of BC, and all over the northwestern US had agreed to focus energy on, and send protection to, Clayoquot Sound at 8:30 p.m. Pacific time. The local contingent took place in the forest at the north end of Chesterman Beach, sheltered from the wind. There were no houses there then.

When the time arrived, we lit some sage and sang a song, something about "blessed be the Earth." We named valleys, rivers, and mountains of the Sound in the east, south, west, and north. I pictured in my mind all the green islands and inlets and mountains. We sang loudly:

> Earth my body, water my blood,
> air my breath and fire my spirit.

We danced, singing about flying around the boundaries of the Sound. As it became dark, we lit a few candles, including a tall white one planted in the ground in the middle of the circle. We spoke of what we most loved about this place. Forests, mild temperatures, beaches, storms, mystery. At the end of the gathering we drew close, arms around each other, finishing with laughter and primal screams!

Soon it was May 1, the pagan holiday of Beltane. Green and I attended a celebration at Ńańak^{w}uʔa. The rain stopped for the whole event, then closed in immediately afterwards. The maypole was a straight cedar branch rising from the sand, its green needles drooping over the top. It was hung with strips of sheets and long ribbons of many colours. There were enough pieces for everyone's hands, and we moved around the pole in a sort of weaving do-si-do while the ribbons shortened, singing:

> We are the flow and we are the ebb
> We are the weavers, we are the web.

After a long time, the ribbons became too short for us to weave any more. It was time to leap over the bonfire with a friend or lover.

All too soon it was back to business, so to speak: I met with my probation officer for the first time, and signed the form that promised I wouldn't go near active logging for a full two years. Quite the challenge to avoid active logging while living on Vancouver Island! The probation officer behaved in a kindly manner.

Someone attempted arson on a Biosphere Project director's shed. (Before Tlaoquiat became a UNESCO Biosphere Reserve, before the Clayoquot Biosphere Trust, there was the Biosphere Project.) And someone poured sludge into a Tlaoquiaht activist's boat's transmission, putting him out of business for several weeks.

We had let marbled murrelet researchers know that we were willing to watch and listen for murrelets where we lived. Stephanie Hughes came to talk to us at the office. The birds were breeding now, and she asked us to spend two days with her in the Sydney Inlet, where she would train us in the art of "Ma Mu surveys." I had my usual fears of bad weather and large carnivorous animals, but was otherwise keen. There was still time before heading out to perform in the travelling play.

Six of us spent all day on an open skiff in terrible weather, pausing for lunch at the mouth of the Megin River. Rapids hurled themselves from between canyon walls into the arms of the equally powerful sea. We ate in the shell of a cabin, where the skipper, Ian, made a fire in an old sink on the floor. We huddled over the fire until someone realized that the floor itself was starting to smoulder. Everyone leapt up and stomped out every last cinder. That was the end of lunch and the beginning of the rest of the day's journey.

After hours of being cold and wet and feeling sorry for myself, the ocean swell increased as we tried to get around the point to Hot Springs village. On top of everything else I started to feel seasick. Our situation didn't seem to bother anyone else. I felt like Eustace on board the *Dawn Treader* in Narnia, before his dragon transformation cure. Stephanie was downright cheerful, chatting away to the guys. Huddled under an overturned canoe in the skiff, I kept hearing her exclaim "Yeah!" "Wow!" and "Great!" When we reached shore the queasiness left me, but other discomforts quickly magnified. We had to climb a rickety ladder to reach a rickety hut. (I did prefer it to a tent.) There was even a woodstove, although it nearly killed us with smoke. Inside at last, Stephanie said smilingly to me, "Isn't this great?" I couldn't even look her in the face. Shivering, dripping, menstruating, nauseous, exhausted, I wondered about the next couple of days. After dinner, naturally, I cheered up a bit. Green and I went to bed. Stephanie and the three other men all went to the hot springs in the darkness and pouring rain.

Thankfully, the next morning brought blazing sun and blue sky. We still had a distance to travel. Our first stop was a bay with three different creeks running into it, where Neil (one of our fellow passengers) had been building a cabin by a giant, moss-covered spruce. There we spread wet clothes out on the rocky beach to dry while all six of us tried to put together a Zodiac. This was what the three of us—Stephanie, Green, and I—would have used to get up the Sydney River. But the floor didn't fit. Ian offered to take us as far as his skiff could go. We had lunch first, there on the beach. The air was warm enough for us to take off several layers of clothing. It was like the day before had never happened.

Soon we were motoring up the long, wide Sydney Inlet. To add to existing clearcuts and road scars on the mountains, there were plans to log all parts of the Sydney that weren't too steep. At present, most of it remains intact, though portions have been threatened by increasingly frequent wildfires.

Mountain after mountain passed by, the forest suspended between each peak in solid sweeps of trees. At last, we were nearing a flat marshy grassland that joined the two sides of land and blocked our way. Two creeks poured forth, one on each side. This was the Sydney estuary.

Neil slipped the pole into the water as we crept slowly forward, to keep track of depth, so the propeller wouldn't touch bottom. A grazing black bear glanced up at us as we approached, and then its head disappeared into the grass again. A couple of minutes later we were closer, and it ran away into the forest. The skiff could finally go no farther; both creeks were too narrow and shallow. Even a Zodiac couldn't have continued. We were dropped off with our packs on the grass.

Ian decided to lend us the company of his dog, Cosmo, to deter bears. A blue heeler, she was dark grey with black patches and huge upright black ears. Her face made me think of a friendly muskrat. She was small, but she had already survived two house fires by burrowing under the house, and saved a man from a charging black bear. Since then I've been taught that dogs can be a bad idea in bruin country, usually running back to humans with a bear in hot pursuit.

We erected our tents just inside the trees next to the western-most creek. Here the sea met with fresh water, and grass met with forest. An estuary: meeting place for the multitude of wildlife attracted to four separate but linked habitats. We couldn't have asked for more. I nearly went into the water, but it was too cold. Green and I stripped off and sat by the river's edge before the sun went behind a hill. All of us tied our food bags onto a rope, slinging them high over a tree branch.

That evening near dusk we sat on a big log under the sky and received our first training session in marbled murrelet detection. The main tools were a hand-held voice recorder, a watch, and a compass. Murrelet detections were one of many details to be recorded. We also monitored time of sunrise, weather conditions, other species detected, and the exact time and direction of discernment. We did not detect any murrelets that evening, just ducks, eagles, and songbirds. There must have been biting insects, too.

Cosmo, however, detected a bear. Growling quietly and trotting away, she reluctantly returned as we whispered firmly after her. The bear, enormous and glossy, emerged slowly from the trees near the eastern brook. She was back to graze at the spot she had run from earlier when we had arrived.

I felt my body tense with fear. But when I saw the bear's face through the binoculars, my anxiety dissolved. She looked cautious, sniffing the air, and moved away from us. She had a gentle expression; I guess that's why I felt she was a she. I felt like an intruder, even an alien, on her home turf. As appreciative as I was to meet with this bear, I was sorry that she was aware of us. She waded through the shallow river and began eating grass on the other side. Our attention was then distracted by a bat.

Stephanie kept Cosmo in her tent that night. I was too nervous to sleep very well and was sure I heard something pass our tent, but could find no prints in the morning. At 5:00 a.m. the world was bright and beautiful under a glowing half moon. A soaring eagle silently brought in the day. As we surveyed, a wind sprang up. It blew a tree down just inside the forest to the north. Moments later, another tree was falling on the hill across the water. "There it is!" cried Stephanie, pointing as Cosmo barked at the echoing creak and groan. I don't know why, but it was eerie to see that tree go down in the middle of all the indifferent survivors.

We heard the murrelets' keer calls a few times. Once, a group of five flew north above the trees, and later one bird winged low over our heads. It was good to have detected these birds in the Sydney, since it was slated for logging, and murrelets are seabirds who nest in ancient trees. Such old-growth-dependent species are, as one might imagine, gravely endangered. If they were protected, with laws behind them, clearcutting here would surely have to be modified in some way! The Ma Mu research group had to stay in the Megin, now protected, because their five-year project was established there before the CLUD was announced.

Once the sun was bright, it was no use trying to detect murrelets, because they tend to be active only when it is still quite dark, avoiding predatory birds such as corvids, hawks, and eagles. It is harder for them to avoid owls. They need to situate their nest under branches to help keep it hidden. After the survey we went back to bed, not waking until ten. Green and I went exploring up the creek at low tide, hoping to reach the end of the flats where the tributaries join to become the real Sydney River. After some time, we realized it could be miles away, and turned back. Curious robins flitted about the branches above our heads.

Soon after we returned to the tents, the skiff arrived and we were heading for home. There were whitecaps, but nothing terrible. Near Tofino a fog set in, obliterating the sky and freezing my bones. After that trip, we recognized keer calls now and again both at home and whilst out and about.

While we'd been gone, there was a meeting in Opitsat between Tlaoquiahts, Ahousahts, environmentalists (FOCS, the Biosphere Project, WCWC, the Sierra Club, Greenpeace, Paul Watson), and media. I was told that apart from Julie Draper (bear protector) for FOCS and Vicky Husband for the Sierra Club, all other speakers were men. Tzeporah Berman told me at the time that we had it good in FOCS. Our group included strong women and worked with equalist principles like consensus and a code of nonviolence. She said that, looking at environmental groups elsewhere, this was not the norm. After the meeting, back on board his ship, Watson fired a cannon. I don't know what his intention was, but the action was inappropriate, considering the burning of Opitsat began with cannons.

One night someone tried to burn a bridge on a logging road. Three local men were caught by a security guard. Everyone I talked to in town felt differently about it.

"How could they have done such a stupid thing?"

"Why didn't they wait until there was no chance of being caught?"

"I don't blame them."

"I guess they couldn't stand it anymore after umpteen years of talk-and-log."

"Won't FOCS get blamed for this? What if the cops frame the Friends?"

"How will this impact blockades? What selfish timing."

"Are you kidding? If they had succeeded, we wouldn't have to blockade at all."

"Naw, a new bridge would be built overnight."

The coming blockades needed high numbers. As Tzeporah told it in *This Crazy Time*, the main bridge burner was someone who had been living in Clayoquot Sound for twenty years. He had "participated in land-use planning, process after process, discussion after debate after study, and while everyone discussed, debated and studied, he'd seen the forest disappear all around him." He'd been on the FOCS board and resigned via his one phone call from lock-up. Tzeporah wrote that, while she understood his frustration, "in a world obsessed with property and consumer goods, destroying property is seen as violent and doesn't help draw people into the fight." The incident put more pressure on FOCS to demonstrate a strategy of peaceful direct action.

Before I departed for rehearsals in Sooke, Green and I took a kayaking class. The instructor went over gear that paddlers are required by law to carry: life jacket, whistle, pump, paddle float, extra paddle. She compared different paddle styles, types of kayaks, ways of getting on board and launching (always bum first), how to steer and turn and correct oneself, how to read charts, what to do with currents and eddies, even how to self-rescue in a wetsuit. All of that in whitecaps!

Grumpy Ann and Painter Jim saw a cougar swimming in Tsapee Narrows. Ann reported that, as she and Jim gently slowed their motorboat, the cat's ears flattened against its head.

THAT DAMN STAGE BEHIND THE RAD

By late May, our first performance of *Fire on the Mountain* loomed. We had costumes and props. Two of the hard hats even had genuine Mac Blo logos on them. And dear Max was part of our crew.

We actors had memorized very little. There were usually distractions during rehearsals, the atmosphere was often chaotic, and some people were merely reading off the page without inflection. Sometimes we seemed to take turns storming out of the room. I was also afraid we wouldn't get through a performance without someone cracking up in laughter. I had joined the troupe because it was an adventure, a means of bonding with friends who lived all over, and a good cause: bringing loggers and ecos together, listening to each other. It was also the best way of seeing the rest of the island. Life was for living. A new experience every day. I failed to spend my youth building toward a lucrative career.

At the opening, Maggie walked onstage and sang this song to set the scene of a blockade:

> There's a fire on the mountain
> and it's the kind not made by wood.
> There's a cold south-wester blowin'
> and it's doin' nobody good.
> There's an ancient stand of cedar
> in this ancient land of rain
> so it's always been there
> and so it shall remain.

The point of our theatre group was to encourage audience participation. The play had a tragic ending of death by fire for both logger and environmentalist: they argued so much about how to save themselves that it became too late to do so. After performing the play, we would invite the audience members to intervene in any way they thought might prevent such an outcome.

In fact, our first show was a success. At 7:30 p.m. Sointula, Malcolm Island, was hushed and still. We figured it was a no-show, and soothed our disappointment by saying, "Well, we can use this time and space for another dress rehearsal." But suddenly a crowd of villagers was quietly walking down the lane to the venue.

After the play, we went through each scene again, but the audience was shy. The only interventions came from cast members. That felt good enough, so we finished and sat down with the audience in a circle. We were told that more people would have come if we had been better advertised. They had all heard by word of mouth. Facebook was still nearly a decade from leaving campus.

There was an article about *Fire on the Mountain* in the *North Island Gazette*, with a quote from the mayor of Port McNeill saying we were "extremists." We were not permitted to perform in his town.

Green was in Tofino helping prepare for a busy summer. I called him on June 7 from a pay phone. He had forgotten his own twenty-ninth birthday.

In Port Hardy, only fourteen people came, but two of them were loggers—smart, friendly, helpful loggers. I felt more for them now. Like we were fighting for people as well as for the forest and its creatures. Everywhere we'd been, the land was devastated, and all suffered while the companies continued to profit at everyone's expense. Share BC folks didn't seem to realize we had a common enemy, but Mac Blo was providing them with food and camping gear, confusing behaviour from an enemy after all. MB gave with one hand (jobs now) and took away with the other (no long-term employment when all the trees are gone).

The village of Zeballos could only be reached by logging roads. (On Vancouver Island, most unpaved roads were logging roads.) A beautiful valley opened up, and there was the village: a single street with houses on either side.

People came across the bridge from the Ehattesaht reserve, left their children with us, and went home! It had been raining, and many kids were shivering without jackets. As soon as one of them was wearing a cast member's shirt, they all wanted to wear our clothes. During the intervention period, the children wanted simply to be *in* the play. So they acted as flames of the fire. Of the twelve adults in the audience, I guessed a couple were teachers from the school. The mayor and his wife thanked us at the end. He said that if he had known what the play was going to be like, he would have made sure the whole village turned up. Would we think of returning for another performance? We stayed at the free campsite despite earlier threats from unfriendly locals. The next morning we were all treated to a full breakfast, offered by an audience member.

Kyuquot was our largest audience yet, made up mostly of Indigenous mums and their lively children; the play took place on their reserve. I had thought Zeballos remote, but to reach Kyuquot you must go beyond Zeballos and travel miles of treacherous logging roads, then take a half-hour boat ride. We saw a bear along the way, and sea otters, rafts of them floating on their backs, munching urchins in their whiskery mouths. Sea otters were once close to extinction due to the fur trade. They still only cover a fraction of their former territory.

Kyuquot was beautiful, but we were shocked to see how much forest was gone. Every island, every mountain was half shaved. I had hoped that this remote place would be as untouched as Wanačis-Hiłthuuʔis. What would be left in another year? However, there was a group: Kyuquot Economic and Environmental Protection Society (KEEPS). They helped us pay for the boat travel. After the gig, Kathy Campsall, who played the environmentalist, told the rest of us funny, twisted stories as we dropped off to sleep on a gym floor.

Fourteen people came to our play in Courtenay, which was a lot better than three in Campbell River. But small audiences could be less nerve-racking for anyone who wanted to do an intervention. In Courtenay, a woman dragged herself onstage as a wounded bird. Our logger character helped the environmentalist tend to the bird. Another audience member had a foul mouth and was very patronizing, ranting at us: Why didn't we do *real* theatre? In the discussion that came afterward, Ruth Masters debated with an IWA executive. I saw that we had succeeded in our goal: getting the two sides talking.

We performed in Port Alberni to members of the Alberni Environmental Coalition (including Bill, with whom I was on trial). Maureen Sager let us camp in her yard. We couldn't get a venue in Ucluelet. The Tofino gig was a dream come true, even though we had expected it: our largest audience of the tour. I didn't count how many. It was in the school gym and the acoustics were awful. I went blank at a crucial point in the Reporter's dialogue with the two loggers. There was a hilarious intervention in which two people ran up and invaded the office of the Company Big Boss; they locked themselves to his desk and his legs and started a revolution. My partner rushed in as a cop. It was anarchy.

After the show, as the cast put away props and changed out of our costumes, there was a spat and one cast member stormed off. We never found him. The show in Nanaimo had to be cancelled. He had made his own way there and was waiting for us, but we didn't know. Cellphones still weren't a thing.

In Victoria, we performed at the Fernwood Community Centre, to a roaring crowd of friends and supporters—and the IWA guy from Courtenay. Rather than intervening, he stood up and made a boring speech before asking us to act out a CORE table scene (Commission on Resources and Environment). Soon after we started, Bobby (the guy who spoke out for moss and murrelets in the Walbran) jumped up from the audience. He cried out, "They want to lure us into all this TALK while they continue to log all the old growth! We won't have it!"

It was pure pell-mellery. At the cue to start the tape of chainsaw noise, Max put funny music on instead. Everyone in the cast got up and started dancing. Bobby and Dan Kerslake (who played the logger) sang Monty Python's "I'm a Lumberjack and I'm Okay" and danced the cancan.

Our last night was a Saturday, in Fernwood again. Afterwards, we all went across the street to a pub for a celebratory drink. We took up three tables, surrounding a middle-aged couple who sat quietly drinking wine. They ignored us. But sharp-eyed Green stared at the man, recognizing him as none other than Dan Miller, BC minister of forests. The secret whipped round the tables in a whisper, making everyone gasp and stare. I couldn't stop laughing; this had to be a forest minister's worst nightmare. And we were getting rowdy.

I yelled above the din, "I love the smell of a clearcut in the morning" (an infamous quote by a Share representative). A guy singing country songs let our Dan and his partner Maggie take the microphone. They led us in Dana Lyons's song, "The Tree":

There's a river flowing near me
And I've watched that river change and grow
For eight hundred years I have lived here
Through the wind, the fire and the snow

I see salmon return every summer
And I watch young owls learn to fly
I have felt the claws of the grizzly
And I have heard the lone wolf's cry

I have seen great glaciers melting
And I've met lightning eye to eye
But now I hear bulldozers coming
And I know that I am soon to die

But who will house the owl
And who will hold that river shore
And who will take refuge in my shadow
When my shadow falls no more?

(Excerpted with permission.)

Dan Miller applauded. So did his companion. He was offered a half-pint of beer courtesy of Earth First! He declined, content with his wine. After a while, we decided to sing "Fire on the Mountain," a rather more defiant and challenging singalong. The minister and his partner got up and left.

Our travelling play was over. It was summer, and I would miss my cast mates. Max was moving into a Victoria house with a Kax-i:ks arrestee. What a packed spring. Little did I know how intense life and the movement to defend temperate rainforests were about to become.

THE SUMMER WE GOT BIG

The word "environmentalist" has already been used several times here. I have always been one, and proud of it; on the other hand, I wish there were no need for the term, because we all ought to be actively caring for the environment. It should be a moot designation. We wouldn't be here without an environment; it keeps us breathing, provides clean waters, grows our food. There should be no separation between those who care and act and those who do neither, or worse. We need to freshen the language to prevent eyes glazing over. My laptop thesaurus offers conservationist, preservationist, ecologist, green[ie], nature lover, eco-activist, eco-nut, eco-freak, tree hugger. But it's just sane. Sanist? Award-winning British author Robert Macfarlane said during an interview that he no longer uses the term "environment." Instead, he chooses "the living world."

To state that 1993 was a historical year in Canada for defenders and protectors of the living world is an understatement. Locals were kept extremely busy while thousands of people came to Clayoquot from around the globe. Many hundreds were arrested for defending these rare and ancient temperate rainforests. People spent weeks and months behind bars for trying to defend precious ecosystems—not wildernesses but ancestral gardens of the living Nuučaan̓uł peoples. Many others organized or participated in actions of support from afar. For a snapshot of what it was like, one could visit YouTube for a Bob Bossin music video, "Sulphur Passage (no pasaran)" or watch the Nettie Wild documentary *Fury for the Sound*.

The spot chosen for FOCS's Peace Camp was known as the Black Hole: a burned clearcut. It was ugly and no doubt embarrassing to Mac Blo, the company responsible. It was also right on the highway, a mile or so from the junction that directs traffic south to Ucluelet, north to Tofino. All the visiting tourists had to drive by us, and this year they would see dozens of colourful flags from supporting countries. They'd stop and check out the information booth. They'd look around at the scorched land and understand why we were there and what we were resisting. Those of us on probation from '92 could help at the camp, because it was more than a kilometre from active logging.

A disadvantage to the site was that, as accessible as it was to tourists, media, police, and ambulances, it was equally within reach to angry and/or inebriated persons who didn't agree with our cause. It was also hot, nearly shadeless, and sooty.

While I wasn't one of the shovel-carrying set-up crew, I was one of many trained peacekeepers at the Make Canada Day Clayoquot Day rally to open the camp. There was no trouble, despite our close proximity to a Share camp. Valerie Langer wrote somewhere that "industry was driving a wedge between the workers and the environmentalists, utilizing the Share groups to do the fear mongering." This time their placards said SAVE OUR COMMUNITIES and WE SUPPORT THE GOVERNMENT DECISION ON CLAYOQUOT. Their ongoing purpose was to block the logging road from forest defenders, while allowing loggers, hunters and fishers through. Hornidge writes in *Loggerheads* about the "great camaraderie" between loggers and police. Loggers "thanked the RCMP and, after work, joined them during evening campfires and BS sessions."

But the grand opening of our Peace Camp was just good music and powerful speeches: Tlaoquiahts Francis Frank and Moses Martin, sustainable forestry hero Merv Wilkinson, Biosphere Project rep David LaRoche, Greenpeace's Karen Mahon, and Valerie for FOCS. Vanessa LeBourdais sang songs from her album *Rainforest Summer*. By the end of the day, over 250 people had arrived.

After that, it was three days before Green and I returned to the camp. I was amazed to see loads of people milling about, mostly faces I'd never seen before. Something electric was in the air. The camp was several times bigger than last year's, and I could tell we were going to be needing all that space. As I stood staring, I heard a familiar voice say "Welcome." It was our friend Paul; he had dug several latrines, a hell of a job in a hardpan clearcut.

We sat in on a meeting, and the number of attendees was impressive. A ritual to renew energy came next. It was hard to be in a circle with both hands held, leaving us all at the mercy of mosquitoes. A song or chant by Gwydion Pendderwen began:

> We won't wait any longer
> We are stronger
> than before
> We won't wait any longer
> We are stronger.

Four people who planned to be arrested the next day stood in the centre. As we sang, we moved in a spiral around them, closing in. When we couldn't wind any tighter, everyone looked around at each other, charged up and bright-eyed. The following morning at half past four, a convoy of vehicles headed out for the Kennedy River bridge. I wished I could have gone along. Three of us (all arrested in '92) were stationed at the front gate with a single handheld radio.

There were about a hundred people at the blockade. After the injunction was read, most of them moved aside, leaving ten protectors standing together. They all wore "My Canada Includes Trees" T-shirts. One of them was Svend Robinson, federal NDP member of Parliament. No police were called in; the company turned back. A triumph. It made national news.

According to my journals, twelve people were arrested on July 6, and the majority of them refused to sign their conditions of release, including two elderly women. One of them, Betty Krawczyk, lived in Ucluelet, so there went the myth of Ukee being a town of "yellow-ribboners"—a term that referred to the local practice of tying a yellow ribbon to a vehicle as a sign of support for logging in Clayoquot and Share BC. Green and I picked Betty up from her home one night and drove her to the Black Hole. I remember the camp discussion about whether or not to sign the promise to stay away from active logging. Betty simply said, "I'm not signing that."

She had owned a cabin up in Cypress Bay. From there she had watched a clearcut grow bigger and bigger until the mountain developed slides that widened and deepened each winter. One day she went as usual to fetch water from the creek near her cabin, only to find the water filthy and choked with muck. She wrote several letters, made phone calls, went in person to the government bodies responsible. After no results, no change, and very little sympathy, she decided she had to do something more. On July 6, she was taken with the others to Port Alberni jail. When the paddy wagons were driving past the camp, dozens of us were ready on both sides of the highway, cheering and waving madly.

On July 7, a father and his two young sons were arrested. Share members stood by, loudly condemning blockaders, as if the kids had had no choice in their action—as if our side had forced them to do it. Harcourt condemned us on the news. I think he even threatened to send in Social Services. The children's views and feelings were not valued. In fact, it was the two boys who had talked their father into coming to the blockade. Raffi, beloved children's entertainer, was interviewed and questioned by the public via a phone-in on the news, regarding the issue of children at protests. He said he believed children have their own minds, feelings, and opinions.

That night, Peace Campers chose a new strategy for the morning: not to engage with Share. Sure enough, at the blockade the pro-logging contingent began hurling their usual verbal abuse to a completely silent crowd of defenders. They soon stopped and looked uncomfortable. There were three arrests that morning.

The next day four people were arrested. One of them was Sile Simpson, who was, of course, on probation from the previous year. This time she was denied bail and faced a $1,500 fine, plus the serious charge of breaching probation—(1) for being there, (2) for blocking logging—plus new contempt charges. Apparently, she didn't sign the form and wouldn't wear the uniform. They put her in solitary confinement until she agreed to wear it. In the end she got the fine plus a six-month sentence. Imagine putting someone away for half a year for trying to halt the destruction of the Earth. Her actions in the long run could benefit the judge who sentenced her, his descendants, the loggers, their children, everyone. *Clayoquot Mass Trials* compared Sile's sentence with the four months given to a man who had sexually assaulted his two stepdaughters from the age of seven. Murderers and rapists were allowed plenty of time to prepare for trial, while forest protectors were not. Mac Blo itself had filthy hands with fifty outstanding charges, while imprisoned grandmothers were not allowed access to a comb.

There continued to be small numbers of arrests every day. These people were constantly supported by large numbers of demonstrators standing on the sides of the road.

Green and I did somehow manage to finish our "Ma Mu" detection training. I was beginning to think we'd never get to the Witness Trail to do a murrelet survey. Finally, we set off in the jeep one afternoon, turning down a logging road at Sutton Pass summit where WCWC sometimes had their information booth. We drove a long way on a rough road, if you could even call it a road. The number of times my head hit the ceiling of the car made me wish for a helmet or a hard hat.

A carved sign stopped our progress. It announced the Witness Trail, which we could see started uphill through more slash. Across the valley was an enormous natural slide, all the way down a mountain. The view looking back from where we had come was awful.

We were in the annihilated Kennedy valley. The river must have been a place of sheer beauty before its violation, but greed had left a waterfall bald and exposed. Stumps, stumps, stumps: sure you haven't left anything, boys? Gotta make a living. Are you sure you don't mean a killing? Why is it that when someone makes a really good living, they call it making a killing?

The First Peoples of this land made their livings for centuries, without destruction. Surely the company workers didn't expect their jobs to last?

It was going to be a solitary hike; Green was dropping me off so he could return to blockade work. I was all set to start when a car drove up; the passengers told me it was a long trek over a mountain. It didn't sound like I would make it down into Clayoquot valley before my food ran out. Green then convinced me to access the valley via another logging road which went right to the edge; I would need only to bushwhack a small distance from there. I agreed, even though we had to go all the way back to the highway to access the other logging road. I was shaken and frazzled already.

As we reached the gate to the second logging road, however, we saw that it was locked. A helicopter inside was carrying cut trees

Info booth, front gate, Peace Camp at the Black Hole. Clayoquot Sound, 1993. Photo: Mark Hobson

from one pile to another, dropping them from the sky like sticks. Green knew of another way in, farther down the highway.

I had been looking forward to immersing myself in the forest, forgetting about clearcuts. I was going there to do my survey and it was good to know there was some intact forest left somewhere. I visualized myself deep in the forest, pouring out all my passions onto paper, holding nothing back.

It was the worst ride of my life. Angular chunks were removed from mountains. Clearcuts crept up slopes, in contrast with forested mountaintops: this was somehow worse than seeing the whole thing shaved. Because I knew their plan was to take the rest. They meant to liquidate it all. Did it know? Did it know it was doomed for the chop? How long did it have? Where would the animals go, and what would become of them?

Incredibly, this road was worse than the first one. Obviously, it was rarely used, so the company hadn't bothered to maintain it. Boulders, fallen trees, and craters were serious obstacles. It went on and on. Desolation clamped onto my heart. I was going to be left at the end of this. At last, we reached the limit of the road. Bushwhacking was impossible. Trees left unprotected by the cutting—trees not used to the winds that whip through clearcuts of any size—had fallen down onto the forest floor. It's called the blowdown effect.

By this time, I was raw, terrorized, and bawling into Green's neck. I couldn't stay, and I couldn't go back and do it all again.

The helicopter was gone. We drove to the gate, a shortcut. Still locked. Panic, just below the surface. We drove to the security guard's camper. As he drove up, a bear ran off up the slope. The guard had the key to the gate. He told us that the helicopter had been "cleaning up" blow-down. Read: harvesting—and profiting from—trees that were meant to be left standing. A sweet deal for Mac Blo, who didn't even have to employ loggers to cut them.

He kindly let us out. We headed straight for home.

⚜

The FOCS office moved from a downtown Tofino basement into Valerie's loft along Pacific Rim Highway. This was our town base, a forty-five-minute drive from the Black Hole. It was a tiny workspace cramping maxed-out staff. Valerie, one of our most eloquent, disarming, and dedicated leaders, no longer had a private home away from camp, where there was also zero privacy and little sleep.

Because the early-morning phone shift started out nice and quiet, that's when I volunteered. I would pick a few mint leaves by the fence for tea before I went in. I would try not to wake Valerie but the ladder to the loft squeaked. The phone would soon wake her anyway. It usually started ringing around 6:45 a.m. Often I hadn't heard from camp yet and would ask the ringer to call back. It was usually radio news people wanting to know the number of arrests. We were in the news every day: radio, TV, and papers. Marlene (Marn) Cummings would call from a pay phone near the Ukee cop shop. Marn turned out to be one of those who "changed her career." A nurse, she later went back to university and landed a master of science in environmental planning. Each morning she made sure I knew the blockade's theme, if any, and provided arrest statistics. A theme might be students or seniors, business people, women and children, teachers, even forestry workers. It was both pleasure and pride to receive Marn's calls. I could then phone media or wait for them to get back to us. By about 9:30 a.m. the circus began and I usually left, to return at suppertime for a couple more hours.

Court-and-jail support was tricky. There was a constant, sometimes frantic search for more lawyers. There were calls from supporters, family members of blockaders, information-seekers making travel and/or arrest plans, lawyers, and trolls, though they weren't named that then. When the *Vancouver Sun* ran an article about ecofeminism at the Peace Camp, we got more phone calls from angry men. Appearances from special guests or celebrities had to be organized. Not by me; I had been an organizer in high school but now preferred answering phones, writing, and proofreading.

Starhawk (author and Wiccan activist) and Joanna Macy (author and Buddhist activist) were coming to the camp on July 20. There would be a women's and children's blockade at that time. And the Australian rock group Midnight Oil were coming to perform.

After countless delays, Green and I were finally able to borrow a friend's boat, and we launched it under Kennedy Bridge one Saturday night. We were going up Clayoquot Arm to attempt another murrelet survey. It took two trips to transport four people and our gear to where the Clayoquot River starts, at the end (or beginning) of the Arm. Kathy and Jenny from *Fire on the Mountain* were with us.

By myself in the dark and drizzle, pitching tents while my partner went to pick up our two buddies, I heard keer calls, which I later recorded as data. I was not entirely alone, however; three young men were working there, cutting fallen cedar for shingles. One was driving a noisy all terrain vehicle. The place had a markedly different atmosphere from the Sydney estuary. There was no grass, just rocks with human litter here and there. It had been logged many years before, and clearcuts were visible on the surrounding mountains. Out of the blue, I missed England.

One of the men gave us the creeps. He stared at Kathy and said, "You're a sight for sore eyes." As a result, we only stayed for one night.

I started my observations at 4:30 a.m. Sunday morning. Sat myself down on a big log with insect repellent, watch, compass, tape recorder, and binoculars. The day's first eagle was soaring above the treetops. A dipper and its darling chick were poking about for food. In the river, a huge salmon died as I sat observing it. I could hardly lift it. There were also a lot of small dead fish which I later reported to the fisheries office in Tofino. I recorded several detections: distant keer calls and two murrelets flying through the air.

On Friday, July 16, there were eighteen arrests. They included the unlawful, obviously RCMP-preplanned arrest of Tzeporah from where she stood on the side of the road—where it was perfectly legal to stand. The authorities were ordering cops to selectively apprehend key organizers. Half of the eighteen arrestees refused to sign that pesky form.

The day and night leading up to the Midnight Oil gig were crazy. We were swamped with four to five thousand people, and many were intoxicated despite camp rules. A few Share people turned up at the front gate. They were instantly surrounded by peacekeepers. I found that my patience was wearing thin, so I left my position.

Another camp had to be set up, near the blockade site. Green and I stayed there with my sister, Beth, in her tent. None of us slept much, thanks to widespread snoring and to the men with drums. They drummed all night. If they knew that people were exhausted from travel or from working weeks to make the concert happen, they didn't care. Drumming was not mentioned in our Peaceful Direct Action Code:

1. Our attitude is one of openness, friendliness and respect toward all beings we encounter.
2. We will not use violence either verbal or physical towards any being.
3. We will not damage any property and we will discourage others from doing so.
4. We will strive for an atmosphere of calm and dignity.
5. We will carry no weapons.
6. We will not bring or use alcohol or drugs.

At wake-up call I had to quickly leave the area (an active logging zone at 6:00 a.m.). Back at the Peace Camp, I found the gate well looked after, so I crawled into Jenny's tent and slept until a sound check from the stage woke me. At extremely short notice, the concert venue had been changed to the Black Hole. FOCS had taken members of Midnight Oil over to Opitsat to meet with the Tlaoquiaht Council and Chiefs. The latter said they didn't feel it was safe to have a concert at the bridge and asked for or recommended it to be moved to the Black Hole. Then several councillors asked the band members to sign their T-shirts with black markers. I love that anecdote.

I soon heard about the blockade, the largest one in Canadian history: three thousand people on the road! MB didn't bother trying to go to work, so no one was arrested. Still, a lot of people felt it was important to stay on the road just in case loggers showed up later. Beth was one of them. She didn't mind missing the concert for that reason.

Midnight Oil's band members had been activists for years already. They had a hit song that demanded to know how we could sleep when our beds were on fire and declared it was time to return our settlers' debt to Indigenous people. The lead singer, Peter Garrett, had been giving rousing speeches to blockade crowds for several days. There is video footage of Garrett speaking to forest defenders. He said that Canadians "ought to be aware that the international community … particularly young people, considers what's happening out here to be a wrong, and are prepared to do something about it."

When I stumbled out of Jenny's tent, it was 8:00 a.m. and camp was jam-packed for the show. I couldn't believe I was about to experience Midnight Oil, live. A group of loggers stood in front of the makeshift stage with placards. One read: AUSSIES, GO BACK TO YOUR OWN BURNING BEDS. As Norleen texted thirty years later, "Jean and I were assigned to be the dancing peacekeepers, blocking their banner. Their energy really changed when the music started, suddenly they were rocking out and having a good time." They had promised Jean they'd be peaceful. She had to hold them to that every so often.

I was dancing with Jenny and Green (who was teary-eyed with

joy) when someone prodded my back. I turned around. It was our own English-Walbranian/Kaxi:ksian, bender-building, Celtic-knot-work-carving, somersaulting, magic bus-driving, Wild Man John back from the UK! He picked me up and whirled me around. We all threw our arms around him. He was carrying an amazing didgeridoo, which he had made himself, of course, from a large ash-tree branch. There were little crystal balls all over it, like something from *The Lord of the Rings*.

I don't recall ever seeing our John after that day, but Pete visited him in Blighty. The teenaged Walbran arrestee Dana, on the other hand, had come to visit the blockade and her mother Grumpy Ann. She meant to look for work in Tofino, but ended up staying all summer at camp, helping to facilitate workshops and trainings. In later days, she was even our roommate for a while.

There is video footage from inside Midnight Oil's car as they left the coast—or tried to. Share and/or loggers blocked, surrounded, and even rocked the vehicle. The band was wedged in. Someone close at hand advised, "Roll up both your windows or you're never gonna get through." Placards read: YOU'RE BARKING UP THE WRONG TREES. SHARE THE CLAYOQUOT. The glass was pounded, angry insults shouted. "Go back to where you came from!" "Roll down your windows and talk to us. You had your say, now let us have ours. What's the matter, you haven't got any balls?" It was not the first time pro-logging folk terrorized vehicle passengers, but I didn't know this.

Our beloved Dana Lyons (not to be confused with Grumpy Ann's daughter) performed at the Black Hole the night after Midnight Oil, on the same waste-wood stage. I love his songs "Turn of the Wrench," "Canada Geese," "Magic," "Big Mountain," "Drop of Water," "The Tree," "Ride the Lawn," "Have to Have a Habitat," "I Am an Animal," and "Love Song to Jane [Goodall]." He is best known perhaps for "Cows with Guns."

❦

Two days later—or nine arrests—I was in the office for twelve hours (6:30 a.m. to 6:30 p.m.) except for a lunch break. Plenty of folks did this far more often than I did; my point is, the time flew by, it was so busy. The constant chatter of numerous voices gave me a grinding headache. Tourists kept wanting to buy our beautiful T-shirts. It was impossible to answer phone calls without countless distractions. I was aware that many people worked for longer on some days. It was easy to lose track of the time when there was so much to do. There were cautions against burnout.

Gathering clippings was a big job. One of the papers, the *Sun* or the *Times Colonist*, had a wonderful picture of the blockade on its front page. It showed the Kennedy Bridge completely clogged with thousands of people holding bright banners and placards. The corporations had to have been quaking in their boots. We still knew the workers were not the baddies here, so in 2023 when a retired logger published his memoir claiming that blockaders often called him "tree killer," I wondered about that. Every effort was made to educate newcomers about things like the Code of Conduct, nonviolent communication, and who the real enemies were—corporations, not workers. But it had to be almost impossible to reach everyone. And it was hard, after all, having anger hurled at us on the daily.

These were some of the messages on the placards, banners, and T-shirts:

CLAYOQUOT SOUND: SAVE WHAT'S LEFT
CLAYOQUOT SOUND NOT CLEAR-CUT SOUND
CLEARCUTTING CLAYOQUOT: STILL NOT SOUND
FOREST INDUSTRY WORKERS AGAINST NON-SUSTAINABLE LOGGING
NO MORE RAW LOG EXPORTS
MY CANADA INCLUDES TREES
CHAINSAW MASSACRE
OLD-GROWTH FORESTS FOREVER
DON'T CUT THE GIANTS
BC JOBS LEAVING WITH RAW LOGS

ON GUARD FOR CANADA
PROTECTORS OF MOTHER EARTH
SHEAR BC
MINING THE FORESTS
NO TREES, NO FISH, NO JOBS
NO JOBS ON A DEAD PLANET
BC FORESTS — A DISASTER AREA. WE WANT A PUBLIC INQUIRY
IF NOT HERE, WHERE?
RAINFOREST RIP-OFF [with Mac Blo logo]
NO PASARAN
WHO GETS THE LAST TREE?
I LOVE CLAYOQUOT SOUND
HOW MANY ARRESTS BEFORE THE *REAL* BAD GUYS ARE CHARGED?

If we were to blockade here today, I would hope for signs declaring:

LAND BACK TO TLAOQUIAHT, AHOUSAHT, HESQUIAHT
CANADA IS ALL NATIVE LAND
RECONCILIATION DOES NOT INCLUDE CLEARCUTTING
DECOLONIZE THE TEMPERATE RAINFOREST
DECOLONIZE THE CLIMATE
IT'S THEIR LAND
LAND CARE, NOT LAND USE
LOGGING OLD GROWTH = FLOODS, DROUGHTS & HEAT DOMES
LOGGING OLD GROWTH = MURDERING WILD SALMON
LOGGING OLD GROWTH = EXTINGUISHING ALL LIFE ON EARTH
ANCIENT RAINFOREST = BREATHABLE AIR + CLEAN WATER FOR ALL

It was a joy to work on a letter from the three imprisoned grandmothers to all Canadian grandmothers. Betty read it to me over the phone where she sat in a Nanaimo prison, and I repeated it into a tape recorder. After pounding it into the computer and editing it, I sent it to every newspaper and all the ministers responsible. My Gram received her own personal copy. Not that she needed converting!

I remember sitting by the campfire waiting for Joanna Macy's workshop "How to Work for the Earth Without Going Crazy!" to start. The sound of a sudden scream did not alarm me. It had the tone of many women releasing their anger together. People around the fire looked at each other and said "Wow." I was grinning, but I noticed some men looking uncomfortable. Then a woman told me what had been happening earlier. At the meeting to plan that morning's women's and children's blockade, one of the all-night drummers had tried to block consensus and prevent such a theme. He was referred to as Iron Ron, after Robert Bly's book, *Iron John*. He said women oppressed men, and that he had been raped by the patriarchy by having to go to work each day. Women who had been sexually assaulted in the past, and other women and men, were very upset by his comment. Several women felt the need for a safe space. They left the meeting and formed a circle near the tree line. That's where the scream came from. Some men had a meeting of their own. After hearing about this, I went with three friends to the women's circle to let them know that Joanna's workshop was about to begin. As I joined their circle for a moment, everyone sang this Z. Budapest / Ian Corrigan verse:

> We all come from the Goddess
> and to her we shall return
> like a drop of rain
> flowing to the ocean.

Back at the fire, Joanna looked frail; she was recovering from pneumonia. She held a microphone and gestured like an evangelist (she was, after all, a teacher of world religions). In early 2024, I searched online for Joanna Macy. Born in 1929, she was still living at ninety-five. But that summer, she suggested to us that we were walking pieces of the Earth—that the rainforest spoke through us. She asked us to feel our heartbeat, to realize it had been with us ever since we were in the womb. (I found this wondrous, as obvious as it may be.) Starhawk was quietly and steadily beating her little drum, and it sounded like a heartbeat. Something that we all had in common. Life, the obvious, the routine, was sacred—a word with baggage, but a word that worked for me then.

We stood up to hold hands and sing. It was a corny song, and I wasn't into it. I quietly complained to Riane, making her giggle. But at the end I felt stoked, wishing I could take part in the actions.

Fourteen people were arrested at the women's and children's blockade (men held a small, respectful circle off to the side).

The following day there were ten arrests including those of Starhawk, her husband, and his three daughters. Before her arrest, the author read from her new novel, *The Fifth Sacred Thing*. The four sacred things were air, fire, water, and earth, being the breath, energy, blood, and body—nothing could live without them, and so they were sacred. No one had any right "to appropriate them or profit from them at the expense of others. Any government that fails to protect them forfeits its legitimacy." The fifth sacred thing was spirit.

Six arrests occurred on the following day. More than eighty in just three weeks.

Green and I were camping in a friend's yard, as our landlords were holidaying in the cabin. There was so much happening that it was getting to me. I would escape by taking Sid or Jazmin to the beach or trail. Thankfully, FOCS had been donated the use of a whole small house for their office, right downtown. I remember how busy it became. I remember taking and delivering phone messages, and asking Margaret Atwood for a donation, and personal disasters in my own and others' lives. I remember poor Shari Bondy coming in one day at 9:00 a.m. to help, only to have me glower at her and say, "We needed you at seven." I had no idea she had been one of the arrested women—the pregnant one—at Sulphur Passage five years previously. They were taken to Oakalla on the mainland. She could have wagged a finger at me and said, "Listen, Missy, I did time in a maximum security prison before you'd ever heard of this place." But she didn't. I remember Tzeporah reading a message out loud: "Evening news interview. Arrive early, for hair and makeup?" She looked at me. "I am in *way* over my head." And I remember jumping up and down when one of the Ma Mu researchers called to tell us that someone found a marbled murrelet eggshell on the Witness Trail.

Starhawk led a spiral dance one evening, on a beach down the highway at Kennedy Lake. To get there our convoy turned onto a dirt road made into a tunnel by arching alder trees. It was lightly raining. Our circle was so big I couldn't hear the voices on the other side. The spiralling went on for ages, and it was hard to keep my footing in the sand. I was so happy and honoured to be there. Food was shared afterwards. It was dark and chilly, but some people went skinny-dipping anyway! There were twenty-one arrests the next morning.

Green and I managed to spend nearly a whole weekend on the Witness Trail. The clear-cut slope quickly led us into the forest, where volunteers were hammering away on the boardwalk. For a long time, we hiked near the big lake. We could see it through the trees. A natural mountain slide enlarged it some years ago, flooding part of the forest. The dead trees—broken-topped, limbed, straight, grey skeletons standing in the water—made an eerie scene.

A warning had been issued that two mother bears in the area were acting aggressively, and one camper had already been charged. Experienced hikers had moved their camp out of the sub-alpine area. I was, naturally, a little nervous. Green kept reassuring me. We hiked for maybe an hour before coming across bear scat deposited in the very centre of our path. I got the message loud and clear.

We reasoned that if we ate all the huckleberries and salmonberries along the trail the bears would have no reason to use it. Suddenly three people came along from the opposite direction. They had been a long way and had not detected any sign of bears. One of them described a flat spot near a creek. We left them, hiked until we found the spot, and pitched our tent there. A rough sign stating "Outhouse" pointed to a hole in the ground. A group of hikers appeared and set up camp just beyond us, so I was no longer nervous. Several metres from our tent we cooked our instant meal on a little stove, and farther down the trail we roped our food up.

It turned out our neighbours were into partying. They made a fire on the rocks and kept me awake. Even worse, my alarm didn't go off, and I didn't stir until 5:40 a.m. I was supposed to have risen before the sun. The mosquitoes were incredibly active on the creek bed, but otherwise the place was magical. I sat with Green where, in the winter, high waters would be rushing and swirling in a fierce current. For now, it was dry rock, dotted with salmonberries, white flowers, purple daisies. I wonder now what those flowers could have been. The purple: aster? I thought we were too late to get any detections, but was thrilled by the distinct sound of multiple keer calls coming from the direction of the Clayoquot valley.

After breakfast, we hiked to the subalpine area, to three lakes. They were each so still: mirrors of the sky. Moss was growing in yellow, brown, red, and every shade of green. It was a little lonely. A grouse was sending echoes all around with its drumming. It sat on a branch right over our path. Its plumage was dark except for its red eyebrows, and it glared down upon us.

The third and highest lake was framed by floating lily pads showing off their large yellow flowers. When the trail began to descend into the valley, and the forest around it thickened, we knew we had better turn back or we'd never make it out before dark.

The grouse was still there. A mist was moving in, alternately covering and revealing surrounding mountain peaks. We were tired and hungry when we reached the tent. As we ate, I could still hear (and fancied I could feel in the ground and trees) the drumming of the grouse. It followed us as we packed up and hiked out.

In a news release, Chief Francis Frank said he would file a court application for an injunction to stop planned logging in the Clayoquot valley, Flores Island, and Hesquiaht territory. Although Harcourt's government had stated the CLUD would not prejudice future treaty processes, the decision affected the very same land and cultural assets to be negotiated.

> We need to protect those lands and resources, not jeopardize our ability to negotiate for them. This decision affects our way of life. We want to protect our children's future. Clayoquot is more than an economic resource to our people.
>
> —Chief Francis Frank,
> quoted in a FOCS newsletter.

When August came, I took part in a demonstration, march, and rally for Clayoquot Sound in downtown Vancouver. It began at 925 West Georgia: Mac Blo's headquarters. From there we marched in the hot sun, pausing on Granville Street near Fletcher Challenge headquarters (where some fabulous drumming took place). Over two thousand of us rallied behind the art gallery. Rousing speeches were delivered to the appreciative crowd, followed by music. I danced with my friends, jumped in the fountain to cool off, and handed out FOCS newsletters.

Meanwhile I visited Sile, who was now on electronic monitoring. She had spent twenty-one days in the Burnaby women's prison. Her application for the leghold trap sat on someone's desk for a week while she was inside. Her sentence of six months was the same length a Mr. Randy Demacedo received for his second time mishandling waste oil transport. According to *Clayoquot Mass Trials*, zero jail terms were handed out following discovery of logging damage to thirty-four of fifty-three Vancouver Island streams.

Logging came to a temporary halt, supposedly due to fire season. Dry days, however, were far fewer than wet ones that summer. Could Mac Blo have pulled out their men ahead of that coming Monday, August 9, of which we had made no secret? Three hundred arrests! As soon as I found out, I needed to do something—anything. I was in North Vancouver, so I phoned the *North Shore News*. They wanted to know if anyone from the north shore had been involved. I didn't know for certain, but I assumed so. Maria and I watched the midday news with Gram. The establishment was scrambling. How else to explain reporters focusing on loggers who talked about blockades "fizzling out now" after such massive civil disobedience? Their focus was directed from someone desperate higher up, someone who had been bought.

There was more on the six o'clock news, including footage of an ex-logger in Ucluelet threatening to break the finger of a guy from the Carmanah Forestry Society. When a young woman took her stand as the first Indigenous person to be arrested on the blockades, however, the media failed to report it.

At the annual Under the Volcano festival in Cates Park, I was permitted to share two minutes on the main stage with someone who spoke about the Walbran. "I'm asking everyone here to come and get arrested for Clayoquot Sound," I said into the microphone, and the audience cheered! Fizzling out, indeed.

Unfortunately, the Walbran hadn't been getting a fraction of the media attention given to Clayoquot. More people heard about the Peace Camp, the big blockades, the big concert, and big names, so they came to Kennedy Bridge, bypassing Kaxi:ks which needed them just as badly. Logging was continuing there as usual.

I got back and noticed arrest numbers reaching daily double digits again. One morning it was mostly Quakers and Mennonites.

I was answering phones in the office when I got a call from a businessman in Ontario. He said he would be sending a $2,500 contribution! Another fine donation came from the author of *Empire of Wood: The MacMillan Bloedel Story*.

One afternoon a yellow-ribbon-flying convoy drove slowly and loudly through Tofino. Two fully loaded logging trucks led the show followed by a few cars and trucks, honking. 3RD GENERATION LOGGER AND PROUD OF IT was painted on a pickup. Everyone in the FOCS office came out to see and be seen by the convoy, but there was no trouble. I found myself waving. Apparently, as the convoy approached the Common Loaf, a local old-timer named Dutch, who had gone to jail for the forest years ago, sat down in the middle of the road, blocking vehicles. Many people joined him.

It was later confirmed that most individuals in that pro-clear-cutting convoy were paid by the companies to do it. There were even threats made to those reluctant to participate!

Straight data: August 16, thirteen arrests. August 17, Youth Day, twenty arrests. August 18, seven arrests. August 19, Seniors' Day, twenty-three arrests, including the oldest at eighty-one. I admit I cried watching that one on the news. August 20, eighteen arrests. And seven arrests each on August 24, 25, and 26.

The Forest Action Network (FAN) had tree-sitters in the Sound, at Bulson Creek. There was excellent media coverage of them being arrested. A woman spoke intelligently and articulately about why she was doing it, and smiled pleasantly as she walked away with the cops. I was so proud of her!

The "Vancouver Stump," an exposé of the *Sun*, was being slipped into mailboxes all over the lower mainland by a secret group. It was wrapped around the real newspaper, disguised as the first section. The "Stump" informed readers that the so-called Forest Alliance, whose largest member was Mac Blo, had hired Burson-Marsteller (BM), the public relations firm, to take care of its image. BM had a special place in hell. The company had worked to whitewash the reputations of Union Carbide (responsible for the lethal chemical disaster in Bhopal, India) and Exxon Valdez (disastrous oil spill in Alaska). BM "issue-managed" Three Mile Island's nuclear reactor failure, and mass disappearances in Argentina. BM covered up genocide in Nigeria. Now it was working for the Forest Alliance, too! Were these histories being taught in Canadian high schools? Are they now? Mac Blo won the right to extend their court injunction for a whole year more.

The bear protectors were sentenced on August 26. Julie got a fine of $100 or five days; Richard got $500 or fourteen days; the guy who returned the bear's hide was fined $1,200 (the value of the hide) with no jail time.

August's last two days marked the beginning of the mass trials in Victoria, starting with 1993's first fifty-one arrestees. In Tofino, we found the FOCS office empty. I had drafted news releases before, only to have Will arrive late, unceremoniously erase my drafts without a glance, and start over. This time there was only me to write and send the releases. They were sweaty-hard work, too.

At 3:00 a.m. on September 1, the phone rang in the computer room where Green and I were sleeping. At first I didn't answer it because I was scared. (Who might be phoning FOCS in the middle of the night?) The answering machine came on, and the next line started ringing. Green remained asleep on his good ear. I picked up the receiver.

A familiar voice explained to me that our convoy of business people coming from Victoria to stand on the road was being held captive on the highway just outside of Port Alberni by angry loggers and Share folks. Business people, after all, had respect and credibility. They couldn't be labelled as welfare bums. These ones supported a ban on clearcutting and were even willing to block the road. They were a serious threat. Valerie was with them, and as soon as she emerged from the bus she was instantly recognized and surrounded. Luckily, no one attempted to harm her. There were several heated discussions, and a bus tire was slashed. All the police did was direct other traffic through.

Two hours later, when it was clear that our convoy would not reach the blockade that morning, the loggers let it go. I was reawakened by the phone ringing again. A radio newsman gave me half a minute's warning before launching into a series of live questions. Still half asleep, I tried to answer him accurately. Later, when the brief interview was aired, I didn't recognize my own voice.

On the logging road, forest defenders from the Peace Camp were prevented from getting to the blockade site by Share.

Of course, the pro-clearcutting blockages gave us more coverage than a simple businesspersons' blockade would have received. One could even say it was the best thing that could have happened. The event took up the first fifteen minutes of the CBC TV six o'clock news. Apart from that day (when no arrests took place), there were twelve protectors arrested each day that week.

Legal matters were becoming a nightmare with a cruel judge, not enough lawyers, anxious arrestees on trial, and rampant burnout. But how could we have known it would be like this? The phone bill alone was $6,000.

Green and I spent a couple of hours at the Clayoquot Days festival, since I had signed up to help sell FOCS merchandise. But I needed respite from crowds. At dusk, I went paddling. The mud flats were covered with gulls, crows and herons. The trees seemed full of kingfishers chasing each other. The water was mirror-still as I watched the moon rise over Hiłthuuʔis. Turning my kayak around to the west, half of the sky was on fire as the sun sank into the sea.

When I looked at arrestee data up to August 13, out of 413 arrestees only eight (4 percent) were unemployed. The age range of those removed from the road by police was five months to eighty-one years. (The old woman came into the office and told me she had done it for her twelve grandchildren.) Eighty-one percent of the 413 were British Columbians. There went the presumptions and the myths: that blockaders were "a bunch of welfare bums," that "they were just kids," and that "they were all foreigners."

We were putting out two or more news releases a day now. I was taking stress vitamins. It was fun to get some laughs showing the bottle around the office. The work could never end because the harder we fought to save our planet, the harder extraction profiteers fought back to continue wrecking it. I sent two articles to the premier with a brief letter. "Why aren't you responding to my concerns about job creation and retraining for loggers, and what is the NDP's stand on Burson-Marsteller?"

On September 5, Vancouver's Commodore Ballroom hosted a musical Friends of the Clayoquot Sound benefit featuring Sarah McLachlan, with Lava Hay, Amanda Hughes, Holly McNarland, Holly Arntzen, Gone Clear, Dadawa, and Ocean Trio. On September 7, over four hundred forest defenders were on the road. Neither police nor loggers came. Share had a press conference in Ucluelet, during which they claimed they were extending the long weekend for an indefinite period. But Mac Blo ordered them back to work on the ninth, and sixteen protectors were arrested that morning. While they had been shut down, Clive Pemberton (logger and local IWA representative) agreed to holding talks with us, but cancelled because we informed the media.

> Native people from Clayoquot Sound are celebrating the UN's Year of Indigenous Peoples by filing complaints with the UN regarding the plunder of their traditional homeland by the talk-and-log policy of the Harcourt government."
>
> —Stephen Hume, *Vancouver Sun*

Suddenly the sun was no longer burning through the fog, and tourists were trickling away. Summer was ending. Heat waves and droughts and smoke did not last through September in those days.

On September 12, I went for a long walk in the forest and found myself dreading my return to the office. It was time to pin up a notice asking someone to take over the early phone shift.

I admitted it: I was cracking. I hated people stopping Green on the street to talk blockades when I was trying to steal him away to the beach. I was losing my manners. I hated the process server's amplified voice as he read the injunction to defenders on videos and on the news. I hated the words of the injunction. I rolled my eyes at the singing. I resented the demand "Are you going to move aside and allow us to go to work today?" I remembered my sister's advice to me when I was eight years old: "Remove the word *hate* from your vocabulary." I was burnt out.

An old roommate sent me information on the Institute for Social Ecology in Vermont. That place did a credit course on Ecofeminist Direct Action. He wrote: "My mum says you are involved in the struggle to save Clayoquot Sound. Thank you. I've been to a lot of places in this crazy world and Clayoquot is the most beautiful place I've seen." Kind words like these never failed to put a lump in my throat. I wondered if he'd ever been to Qwabadiwa territory, Kaxi:ks river. I was going to suggest he take that trip.

PADDLING VS. PIMPING

We were back in the cabin on Stockham. There seemed to be more cormorants, herons, and ravens than before. Red-shafted flickers were plentiful. Swainson's thrushes were here only for one precious month or two in early summer. Unless I recorded when I first detected a creature, and then made a note of when I stopped hearing or seeing it, I couldn't be sure of how long it was with us. As for the Swainson's, I've loved its spiralling song since I was a child. In 1991, I had finally learned its name by listening to a tape purchased in the Wild Birds Nature Shop in Vancouver. We were at Beth's, lying on the couch, when the narrator announced "Swainson's thrush." As soon as I heard the bird's song I cried "THAT'S IT!" Poor Green had been half asleep and nearly had heart failure. I have only ever seen a couple; they are very shy and their dull plumage camouflages them well. They seem to show up in all of my books, however. Tlaoquiahts call it the Summer Bird.

Harcourt shuffled his cabinet that autumn. He replaced Dan Miller with a new forests minister, Andrew Petter, who supposedly had sympathy towards "environmentalism." I heard Valerie's voice on the radio at 5:20 a.m. one morning. She was optimistic, so we were too. Unfortunately, he turned out to be another pimp for industry. At a cost of $75,000, Petter went on a ten-day tour to Europe about a year later to promote BC clear-cut timber, scold environmental activists, and tell lies.

Tree-sitters from FAN still occupied a couple of trees at the end of a logging road in the Bulson. Media and police were not strangers to the situation, since Mac Blo employees threatened to blast at the foot of the trees.

An opening ceremony for the Big Trees Trail took place. Opitsat people had covered the trail from the water to the Hanging Garden Cedar with a boardwalk. While the work had been in progress, the trail was closed to the public; many feet stomping on it over the years had worn it into a quagmire. The parts I remembered as steep and difficult were now covered with sturdy steps. It was fun being a part of the appreciative crowd of mostly locals, giving the boardwalk its first public use.

The trail had always been a major tourist attraction. Many of its trees are breathtaking. The Hanging Garden Cedar is its own ecosystem. It's an ancient cedar with much younger hemlock and other species growing from it: a vertical nurse log. All the plants that make up the bottom layer of a forest are growing from its trunk, some at a great height: salal, ferns, huckleberries. And, it's hollow: children and adults crawled inside and stood up. Nowadays, though, it is off limits to the public for good reason. Humans were wearing it out. But when you are in a rainforest and you look around, a lot of ancient trees could be described as hanging gardens after all.

On Monday, September 27, 1993, after thirteen more arrests, we passed the seven hundred mark.

In early October I was telling my Gram about all the pileated woodpeckers I saw on a recent cycling trip to the Gulf Islands, and she was delighted. But suddenly she sobbed: "That makes me want to cry!"

"Why?"

"Oh, because they're going to cut it all down!"

"No."

"Yes, they are," she said. "They're cutting Galiano."

Various companies were, as it turned out, clearcutting private land on many of the Gulf Islands, levelling forests in preparation for housing developments. They had groups of angry residents to deal with—hopefully not with more SLAPP suits.

Inevitably, our conversation turned to Clayoquot.

"I'm so frustrated. I can't do a damn thing. I can't even walk anymore, Chris." She explained that she'd been a socialist all her life, and now that there was a movement she wanted to be a part of, she couldn't really do anything.

Gram did, in fact, do lots. She wrote letters to elected representatives and gave me unwavering moral support. She was never afraid to get on the phone to any politician and give 'em a piece of her mind. To this day, I don't know anyone with the guts to phone government out of the blue like that. When she was younger, she attended demonstrations and community meetings, despite having four children. She was an active member of the NDP. She was never afraid to talk about controversial issues with anyone, even if they strongly disagreed with her views. *Especially* if they strongly disagreed with her views.

She brought up the subject of my uncle, her son John. He worked for Hollyburn Lumber at the time.

"He feels bad about it sometimes, Chris. But it's the best job he's ever had. They saw him through his operation. And he's got a dental plan; he's had all his teeth fixed."

I pointed out that his job did not result in the exporting of raw logs or under-processed wood. The more people in BC who work in any form of secondary manufacturing, the less often ancient forests will need to be cut for the sake of jobs.

"Yes, but it's still old growth," she said.

One day, he had told her, the subject of blockades came up at work during a break.

"Well, I have a niece up there who's been arrested and done her time," he said.

There was dead silence, and gradually everyone went back to work. Later, the boss walked back to my uncle and said, "Y'know, I don't think they should be cutting those trees either."

Gram would be turning eighty-six in a couple of weeks. I asked her what she would do if she were able.

"I would add myself to the numbers," she said firmly. "I'd get arrested."

> These giant trees have stood and sustained other lifeforms, including us, for ages uncountable—the largest living beings evolution has ever witnessed on this planet. Now we all stand on guard for them. The price we pay is small, so small, for the debt of gratitude we owe them. I would be guilty of negligence, criminal indeed, if I did not do everything nonviolent I could to save them as they have so often saved me. … We have brought a violent crime called clearcutting into worthy disrepute.
>
> —Arrestee Robert Light

Back in Tofino, I slept in the office Sunday night, and the phone started ringing around 6:30 a.m. on Monday morning. About five hundred people were on the bridge, and Mac Blo didn't turn up.

The now legendary Peace Camp was dismantled. It had survived numerous attacks by drunk and/or violent adversaries, countless long meetings, stress, conflict, some misogyny, numerous outhouse relocations, sleeplessness, and one major storm of wind and rain. It was run by heroes, visited by many beautiful people who inspired each other to carry on, and is now a part of history.

On CBC Radio, Mac Blo admitted that they were cutting as fast as they could because they knew they wouldn't be able to log this way much longer.

> The summer of 1993 represents, in many people's minds, a time when the NDP government of British Columbia embarrassed itself internation-

> ally by allowing transnationals MacMillan Bloedel and Interfor access to 74 percent of the ancient forests of Clayoquot Sound. They persecuted the very citizens who were once party supporters and stubbornly refused to call a moratorium on the clear-cut destruction of the largest tract of lowland coastal ancient temperate rainforest on this planet. Twelve thousand people showed up on the logging road last summer, outraged by the actions of the government and logging companies. International concern about Clayoquot Sound, forest practices in Canada and treatment of First Nations people has grown immensely.
>
> —FOCS Spring/Summer 1994 newsletter

We boated to the cabin from town one October night, under the stars. After docking, we stayed in the boat and watched the sky for a long time. A shooting star crossed the Milky Way in a second. The spaces between stars were tum̓aqƛ̓, pitch black, and tree branches were like ravens' wings. The reflections on the water were mesmerizing: a dark mass, an island, separated two spheres of stars—twinkling above, in that dome of space, and twinkling below, on the smooth ocean. The stars, in effect, met around the island and made a circle. We could have been in outer space but for the slight movement of our boat. It was incredibly quiet. Looking over the edge, we saw white sparks of bioluminescence created by small eddies in the current.

Our tranquility was broken by river otters surfacing under the dock. We held our breath. They snorted and splashed underneath the boards. I think one climbed up on top, with a pitter-patter of otter feet, but it was too dark to know for certain. As soon as I thought I heard it, there were several splashes, and five short streams of glowing luminescence moving away. We went in then, leaving the dock empty for them to return if they wished.

On another day a friend and I went for a relaxed paddle. A beautiful female kingfisher flew tight circles around us. Two eagles interacted in the air over our heads: one would turn upside down in midflight and, with its talons, aim a strike at the other.

That night at the school after Garth's slide show, video footage of various blockades over the summer was shown. Nansi and I were giggly, having seen this stuff so many times. Oh yes, eyes rolling, yet another writhing mass of people on the road being read the injunction. "Glad my probation prohibited me from being there and having to listen to that every day." Arrest after arrest after arrest, day after day after day (yawn). But suddenly, I *saw* what we had been watching. The summer was truly incredible. The headline on our latest newsletter read: "750+ ARRESTED." And we weren't finished.

Norleen Lillico and Julie Draper were driving to Nelson; I went along to see autumn colours and new-to-me places. We arrived at 9:00 p.m., in time to join a Clayoquot benefit. Nearly every seat in the theatre was full. There was music, comedy, and dance. The "Stump Tour" was part of this variety event. WCWC was taking a giant stump across Canada to Ottawa, in time for the election and a demonstration on Parliament Hill. The ancient stump was taken from a clearcut near the Clayoquot Valley Witness Trail. We stayed with the woman who ran the Grizzly Project. I had a nightmare in which activists I knew were being crucified and burned.

While we were away, we stayed in touch, so we knew there were thirteen more arrests on October 12. The theme was university students. On our long way back, we stopped at a pay phone. That's how we learned that the first forty-four defendants of the 1993 blockades had been sentenced to forty-five days in jail—with no option of electronic monitoring—plus fines of $1,500 to $2,500. A Tofino doctor got sixty days plus $3,000. The judge was punishing people for their behaviour in his "kangaroo court."

According to *Mass Trials*, "The trial was tumultuous, feelings were frequently vented. There were tears, cries, murmuring, laughter, even applause. A mass of people, without lawyers, in court for the first time, was a recipe for mistrial. Every spectator seat was in demand." From Judge Hutchison of a later trial, quoted by Roger Stonebanks in the *Times Colonist*: "The defendants were 'exemplary in every way,' in the courtroom and were respectful and polite." Most of the convicted were now out on bail, appealing, while some remained inside.

Julie drove me to North Van. Gram opened her front door holding a photo she had clipped from the front page of the *Vancouver Sun*. It showed a heart-wrenching scene of defenders on the courthouse steps after hearing their sentencing. In the crowd, two very young women in white dresses held each other in shock. In the background, Sally Sunshine—the blockade's truest flower child, a middle-aged mother from Salt Spring who loved everybody and always wore a smile—for once looked as though a storm cloud had passed over her face. The news also made the front pages of the *Times Colonist*, the *Province* and the *Globe and Mail*.

I travelled from Gram's to the Victoria courthouse, where there had been a twenty-four-hour vigil in support of Clayoquot defenders. Tents were pitched all over the grass along the sidewalk. While there, I learned of accidents in the Walbran. A rope used to hoist a tree platform snapped and hit a man's eye. A young woman fell down a deep crevice, and Mac went down after her, causing a bit of an avalanche. The two of them huddled on a cliff edge all night.

Back in the Sound we arose at 4:30 a.m. and I was dropped off at the office. The business people had returned from Victoria. Never mind having been held captive by angry loggers—even stiff prison sentences did not deter more arrests! Eleven people were taken by police in the darkness and pouring rain. As Valerie wrote in 1994's *Witness to Wilderness: The Clayoquot Sound Anthology*, "Jail is not a deterrent to civil disobedience; social and political change is."

Soon after that, I was kayaking into town against wind and tide to vote in the federal election. The Liberals got in, and Jean

Chrétien was the new prime minister. He had spoken about putting Clayoquot Sound into the national park system, as part of Pacific Rim. Of course, his words were changing now that he was in power: the final say remained with the BC government—which already had its say in April on Naćaas.

I went paddling in the fog (against the current again) to the Big Trees Trail. Four Tlaoquiaht men were putting finishing touches on the boardwalk at the edge of the water. After chatting with them a bit, I headed steadily for the first mammoth cedar, a tree which never ceases to amaze me. More eventful was my paddle home from town the next night at sunset. I wanted to just go for it, even though it was getting dark and I was feeling a bit nervous. Just before Stockham, I thought of porpoises. Then I heard them—the thrilling sound of that swift letting-out of air followed by the sharp intake of breath before the animal submerges again. Suddenly they were all around me in the sunset, impossible to count. One came thrillingly close, about two kayak-lengths away. I called softly to it in greeting, and sang a little, remembering Norleen saying she had been singing lustily when they approached her. But I wanted to be still, to watch and listen. Three of them kept coming up single file, one breath after another, a synchronized movement of three fins on three curving, black backs. They didn't have to stay in that area. I like to think they paused specifically to check me out, before carrying on. They literally swam off into the sunset. I dragged my heavy boat up the trail, draped in moonlight, and stumbled home through the bushes.

Another time that fall, not until I was motoring through rough chop from Stockham toward the other islands did I realize I was in trouble. I reached the calm in the middle of the three islands: Tibbs, Beck, and Stone. I should have turned back then, but didn't want to spend the night alone, so I moved slowly past the oasis of those islands, into turmoil. White waves seemed to go on forever, even though Tofino harbour does not. I was scared enough to try going faster at one point, but nearly lost hold of the wheel. Jerking the throttle back again, I found myself praying out loud in a whiny voice. It was more like a pathetic begging. I was hardly breathing until I made it to Jensen's dock, and was shaking so much that I could barely tie up. Why hadn't someone warned us before we moved? Lesson learned: turn back. Better yet, know which way the tide is moving first, and if a gale-force wind is moving against it, stay home.

Trying to get five friends over to the Big Trees proved difficult one day. I grounded the boat on a mud flat, and then crashed into a rock that was just below the surface. I thought we were going to sink. Pete, who was visiting, said: "Next time we hit something, we'll crack like an egg."

At the Hanging Garden Tree, two eagles made their close presence known to us with their calls, louder and more beautiful than ever. They were perched on top of a nearby spruce. Everyone took turns looking through the binoculars. It was worth all the fright just for that.

Then Amy saw a cougar in her driveway at 9:30 a.m.!

On yet another day Pete and I went paddling over to the Arakun Islands. He loved it. He would pass a piece of floating kelp and cry, "Hello, Kelp!" To which the kelp would answer, "Hello, Peter!" in a high-pitched English accent, so it came out more like "Peteuh." A cliff face had icicles hanging from it. The setting sun cast a beautiful tangerine light in patches onto foliage.

After his departure I took the boat out to look at geese, and ended up feeling awful because I scared them off. Hundreds, maybe thousands of geese filled the sky, moving farther and farther away with their cries of alarm. I learned, or relearned, that it's always best to stay well back and watch through binoculars or a scope. Motorless vessels are ideal. Wild birds travel across the globe to reach these mud flats and beaches. They are tired and famished. Any extra stress (like being chased by kids or unleashed dogs) can kill them. It's why Tofino's Raincoast Education Society eventually started the campaign to Give Shorebirds Space on the Beach!

BBC Wildlife magazine published an article comparing Clayoquot to Twyford Down, where the British government was ignoring the European Economic Community, of which it was a part, by cutting a highway through rare chalk downland habitat. I appreciated the comparison. In Britain, they were degrading an ecosystem and making life very hard for the creatures who belong to chalk downlands. Some butterfly species already in danger could be worse off due to the new stretch of highway. The British government was also lowering its citizens' standard of life by invading one of the very last undeveloped places in that entire road-scarred country. In Canada, we were doing all of the above, but with vastly larger areas. Our government and logging companies were also destroying Earth's lungs, the forests of North America, proper name Turtle Island.

In early November, we were in Victoria again. Sentences were handed down: suspended jail time and fines. They were less draconian since the mass public outcry over the first sentences. I stopped by the Clayoquot Resource Centre. Busy, busy, busy, full of people who were not burnt out!

Over the strait in Vancouver, we attended The Great Clayoquot Sound Writers' Reading and Literary Auction. A daytime event at the Commodore, it was "billed as the most prominent gathering of writers ever to assemble in one venue in the service of an environmental cause." Tickets were only $12.50. The late Pierre Berton was master of ceremonies. Susan Musgrave was in Tofino and her car wouldn't start, so she was unable to join her co-host William Deverell. But her donation to the auction was already there: French garters that set off a prison alarm at her wedding to bank robber/novelist Stephen Reid. The second part of the event was co-hosted by Myrna Kostash and John Gray. The list of readers and speakers, some no longer with us, was a who's who of CanLit: Joy Kogawa,

Al Purdy, Audrey Thomas, Stan Persky, Lillian Allen, Lee Maracle, Peter C. Newman, Patrick Lane, Lorna Crozier, Herb Hammond, Brian Brett, Marilyn Bowering, and surprise special guests. This is all off the poster, which is on my wall after being stored in a tube for two decades. I unearthed it a couple of years ago, to my surprise and awe. There is also an image of it (and a chapter about it) in *Witness to Wilderness*.

Auction items like limited first editions and art were donated by many, including Margaret Atwood, Robert Bateman, Brian Brett, Robert Bringhurst, Douglas & McIntyre Ltd., Timothy Findley, Charles Lillard, Farley Mowat, Toni Onley, P.K. Page, Linda Rogers, Joe Rosenblatt, Jane Rule, Bill Reid, Press Gang Publishers, Jack Shadbolt, Robin Skelton, Jack Wise, and George Woodcock.

I remember feeling warmed by Al Purdy's unpretentious reading. Bill Reid, the Haida artist, was pushed to the microphone in a wheelchair. I recalled watching him years earlier, in 1989, carve an enormous sculpture in his workshop on Granville Island. It was *Spirit of Haida Gwaii / the Jade Canoe*. He had already been suffering from Parkinson's disease for years then. I couldn't make out most of what he said on the Commodore stage, but I was in tears anyway. He got two standing ovations.

Among the various tables was one displaying Mac Blo propaganda, with two public relations people talking to the crowd and media—this pair could have been the Burson-Marsteller contingent, I realize now. Mac Blo donated for auction a helicopter ride over the saved areas of the Sound (as if MB had anything to do with saving Clayoquot!). How the pilot hoped to avert people's eyes from miles and miles of clearcut moonscapes, I didn't know.

Valerie successfully bid for a wooden dummy of Harcourt holding out a donation box. Farley Mowat's pipe went for a good price. Even U2 donated something. At the end, Pierre Berton auctioned off his tie. The show made $22,000, which was to be used to pay arrestees' fines (there was talk of an ad, too). Back then, that was a nice amount of cash. And it's still more than I make in a year!

⁂

Greenpeace had been carrying out several different actions. They had tree-sitters (banner-hangers) and a blockade, both at Kennedy Bridge on Tuesday, and eight people were arrested. Some were international Greenpeace reps from England, Australia, and Germany. They were attached to cement stumps for several hours. This was and is how crucial Canadian temperate rainforests are to the planet. It made sense that defenders from near and far would care so much.

That might have been the same day the Clayoquot Express arrived—a trainload of protectors that started from Newfoundland, making stops across Canada, with the tag line "From the ocean without fish to the forests without trees." Tofino showed its appreciation by holding a potluck dinner and slide show. Wednesday was their blockade. Finding myself working in the office again, I wrote the news release. A few days later we voted in the municipal election. At an even younger age I had read about anarchism and warmed to it. But to give up voting? Before women were granted the vote, they had to fight for it. Some even died for it. I couldn't disregard their sacrifice.

And the election was interesting. In this village, there was so much more at stake than common issues (not that Tofino Council has much power over the fate of Clayoquot Sound). At the all-candidates meeting the logging issue was mentioned only once, near the end. I think everyone wanted to believe we were one big happy family with plenty of common ground, and to speak of logging would ruin the warm, fuzzy feeling in the room. Or, maybe certain councillors and candidates didn't want it mentioned for other reasons. People kept saying how awful polarization is within the community. This complaint led Valerie to write an article for *The Sound* about polarization being a healthy, necessary element on the path to justice and change.

Tofino Council had been made up of two "greens" and four "rednecks" but the election results evened that out to three and three.

⁂

Provincially, elected Chiefs of the Nuučaan̓uł Tribal Council struck a deal with Harcourt. They stayed up all night—after weeks of negotiations—and at 5:30 a.m. signed an agreement to "comanage" Clayoquot Sound. It was called the Interim Measures Agreement (IMA). A WCWC news release stated that this was "not a cutting plan, but a process of land use decision-making." A spokesperson was quoted: "The agreement is based on principles of conservation, including 'the responsibility to preserve and protect [First Nations'] territories and waters for generations which will follow'. ... Specifically the agreement requires that all culturally modified trees (CMTs) in Clayoquot Sound must be protected and that they cannot be cut without the First Nation in whose territory the tree is found gives permission [*sic*]. ... It also states that, in Clayoquot Valley, for example, logging cannot proceed unless MacMillan Bloedel can prove that there is no possibility of any adverse effects of logging on the Clayoquot River system."

The WCWC release also said that, five days after the Interim Measures Agreement was signed, the Nuučaan̓uł Tribal Council had submitted their request to the federal government to proceed with treaty negotiations. And "widespread public confusion" meant "many people were thinking that natives will now have their own logging shows in Clayoquot Sound." But "First Nations' training will be of a different sort than just learning how to cut down and haul out the trees."

For many years now Gisele Martin, Tlaoquiaht woman, has been pointing out that the term "land use" should be replaced by "land care."

Garth presented a well-attended slide show of his Japan tour. I knew the facts, but to see photos of Clayoquot lumber stacked on Tokyo docks still shocked me. The next morning, I took Sid to the beach, and saw men and trucks working to widen the dirt road through the forest for the new resort at North Chesterman.

In late January 1994 I was busy proofing the FOCS newsletter, yet managed to go paddling twice. Green and I visited an old settlers' graveyard on a small island. We beached in a quiet little bay and easily found the trail. It was a narrow clay path, framed by countless lush ferns. We had to duck under thick salal in some places. The headstones were growing moss that framed the words engraved to remember the dead, or it partly covered them, or it obliterated them. The forest was taking back this boneyard, reclaiming its ground. There was one small, white wooden cross stuck into the soil, deep in tangled dead salal or salmonberry. We almost didn't spot it. There was no name on it. We sat on some rocks and admired the still green water as the misty drizzle nurtured the moss on the graves.

How hard it must have been to transport headstones, especially before the road. Most of them dated from the 1920s and '30s. The oldest one said 1909; this was two years after Gram was born. A few names were Norwegian and Japanese. Some graves had fences around them. A Japanese one, complete with fence and wooden tombstone carved in Japanese syllabary, had fake flowers in a glass or plastic ball next to it. In 1947, Tofino excluded "all Orientals" from its municipality. Ucluelet shares no such shame.

Paddling back, we hugged shorelines, catching sight of a kingfisher diving. It snagged a shiny fish and swallowed it whole. A pair of perched eagles was surrounded by crows. Every treetop was occupied! Nearing home, we found three Opitsat boys with their rowboat on a rock, pulling up a crab trap. They chatted with us for a while. A seal looked at us; one of the boys shouted "Bang!" at it, pointing his hand like a gun. Suddenly a deep, ominous blast came to our ears. Road building in the Bulson valley. Would it ever end? That was neither the last nor the loudest we were to hear that winter.

Fog was threatening to roll in. The boys said goodbye and quickly set off rowing home to their village. We reached Stockham beach at sunset and the sun broke briefly through. We didn't land right away because a flicker was pecking away at the big drift log. Sounds of geese distracted us; a flock was coming across the sky due south. When it was gone, a much larger flock materialized out of the cloud cover, approaching from the east and turning south.

In North Van again, I walked into David Schreck's office on Lower Lonsdale. He was the region's MLA. I spoke to his receptionist about the latest grannies getting strip-searched, but she just spewed the party line. In fact, it was hard for me to get a word in. Finally, I told her that I happened to live in Clayoquot, that I could hear the blasting; every day logging continued on the same giant clearcuts and road building in at least two areas of the Sound. She was surprised. Could they at least stop while the new code was being put in place? I asked. She agreed to report to Schreck when he came in.

Next, I walked up the street to the new "community police office." There was a volunteer receptionist there, and no cops. She said the same thing as the other woman: that it's probably routine to "search" inmates for potentially harmful objects. I replied, "But Clayoquot grannies, having to 'spread their cheeks'? There is no excuse for this." She suggested I go to the police headquarters up on Thirteenth Street. I was on my way to the seabus. I decided not to walk uphill for ten blocks in the opposite direction.

She even said that dead trees needed removing or "they'd all fall down." If that were true, the forests would have been horizontal when the first settlers arrived, and the latter would have had a lot less work to do! The hubristic myth persisted of original forests being naturally regressive without our drastic intervention.

Meanwhile, Harcourt was in Europe, pimping for the industry: spending taxpayers' money spreading lies that BC forestry was improving. He took an Indigenous man with him. Greenpeace was demonstrating over there and might back off because of this man. But he wasn't Harcourt's only company; Tzeporah was there, publicly debating with the premier.

The Friends of Clayoquot Sound's mission statement now read thus: "To be peaceful, courageous, and consistent advocates for the protection and restoration of the ecosystems of Clayoquot Sound, with respect for the *Ha-houlthee* of the *Ha-wii* (the traditional rights and responsibilities of the hereditary Chiefs)."

Sometime on February 9 or 10, Interfor spilled up to one thousand gallons of diesel in Stewardson Inlet, Hesquiaht territory. The diesel ran into a creek and ended up in the ocean. After the Department of Fisheries and Oceans placed booms, gravel, and hay bales, then departed, a crew of Hesquiaht men spent two and a half days cleaning up soaked and reeking natural materials and logging debris in an area of beach over forty-five metres long. It looked "like a river of diesel." Interfor offered to pay the men $15 an hour.

One evening it was already dark when I told Green via the radio not to come home. Snow was flying horizontally past the kitchen window. But he headed out from town anyway, hit a rock, wrecked the new propeller, broke a pulley, and scraped the bottom of the boat. Lesson learned. He docked at our neighbour's and walked home from there. None of the snow stayed on the island, but Tofino was covered, as were its beaches. I had just been dreaming of hummingbirds, a mother and her tiny babies, perched like jewels on my fingertips.

It tires me out now to remember all the travelling we used to do between Tofino and the lower mainland. At the end of February 1994, I was at an ecofeminist forum at the University of British Columbia. Feminism to me is another word for equality. I scribbled a quote from Susan Griffin's "Split Culture": "Long ago we gave up ourselves. … We have traded our real existence, our real feelings for a delusion. Instead of fighting for our lives, we bend all our efforts to defend delusion. We deny all evidence at hand that this civilization, which has shaped our minds, is also destroying the earth."

To open the forum, Amy Simpson introduced the speakers

and offered a definition of ecofeminism from Carol Adams's book, *Ecofeminism and the Sacred*. Tzeporah, in the *Clayoquot Perpetual Diary*, defined it thus: "Ecofeminism is a theory, a life practice and a movement for social change, through which the connections between the domination of Nature and the oppression of women in patriarchal society is explored and validated."

Stephanie was there and read a beautiful description of a typical night spent high up a tree on a platform, observing wildlife and surveying for murrelets, and how in the morning she would stretch as the forest creatures do, toward the sun's first rays.

Jean McLaren reminisced about her busy role at the Peace Camp, and a woman who grew up in a logging community told us of her own experiences. Sushil Saini did some fabulous rap poetry about sizeism (or weightism/fat phobia) within the women's movement, and about a misogynist who had recently been fired from the Clayoquot Resource Centre.

Gisele Martin was sixteen at the time. She told the audience about her trip to Europe, where she stood with her father Joe at the United Nations in Geneva as he made a presentation to the conference on the International Tropical Timber Agreement. She wasn't sure what else to say to us, so she asked for questions. What stood out for me was when she said that we don't appreciate the simple things in life; we take things for granted. "A glass replenishes us when we are thirsty time and time again, yet to us it is just a tool, a slave." Years later I joined her people in a march to Tofino from Esowista, protesting the lack of clean drinking water on that reserve.

In 2023, I attended one of Gisele's many presentations to tourists. Among other terms, she taught ii-saak-sin-hi-in, or "Let us be respectful, observant and appreciative of Natural Law." She taught yuuts-hap-sin-hi-in, or "Let us behave with honour, dignity, respect and humility." She taught qwa-siin-hap-in, or "Let us leave things as they are. Avoid disturbing, destroying or removing Indigenous plants, animals, shells, stones, & minerals." She taught tiich-siin-hi-in, or "Let us protect life by staying safe, being prepared and by supporting the continuation of life for generations to come." She taught taa-quuqh-lthi-in, or "Let us speak truthfully and act honourably." Let us learn the history of this place and its People, correcting colonial narratives like the myth of wilderness. An intact rainforest or other natural ecosystem is unurbanized, yes, and unindustrialized. What we've been used to calling wilderness has never been commercially exploited, but it is not unfavoured, forgotten, or feared wasteland. And in this time of climate breakdown, unurbanized spaces are crucial to Earth's carbon budget. You'd think exploiting them for short-term gain would be outlawed.

WELCOME TO THE STRUGGLE

It is often said Tofino exists in a bubble. That we must cast our gaze outward, at least momentarily, to catch a reality check or gain a little perspective. In April 1994, South Africa held its first multiracial elections. I had attended Free Nelson Mandela rallies in England, and had seen flames licking up the facade of the South African Embassy during the Poll Tax riot in Trafalgar Square. Mandela was released from prison in 1990 after twenty-seven years inside. Now he was to become president of his country.

In June of 1994, Tzeporah's trial began. A cop had told her "the police are working with MacMillan Bloedel to build the case against you." Tzep and Valerie gave excellent speeches at a vigil and rally. The outrageous charge was 857 criminal counts of aiding and abetting those arrested. I held a sign, possibly made by Ruth: AIDING AND ABETTING THIS PLANET.

A top lawyer volunteered as defence. Tzep never had to sign the promise not to return to the blockades. But she faced six years, more than some violent felons and child molesters were getting. Ultimately, a judge, after hearing four days of Crown counsel evidence, threw the case out on a no-evidence verdict.

Harcourt made a major TV announcement pledging to stick with loggers (and logging) no matter what. In reality he was sticking with the company, with his financial investment there, and with clearcutting. I recall him making an appearance as close as Port Alberni, and Garth going down to speak. I wondered if Garth would get mobbed, or his tires slashed. I don't recall how that turned out. By July, our oldest arrestee, Summer Pemberton, was eighty-two and dying of cancer. FOCS organized a card. When I signed it I tried to express how much her arrest meant to me, and told her a little bit about Gram.

Then on July 5, FAN did an action at Lost Lake. The workers cut around a tree-sitter—risking his life—and went to work. Later he came down to make a run for it, but was caught, intimidated by loggers, and finally arrested.

I think it was July 16 when Tin Wis threw a day of celebration: speeches, ancestral drumming, dancing, and singing. I felt so privileged to see the dances, the patterns of art on traditional clothing, and to hear ceremonial drums keeping time to strong voices chanting.

Following this was a week-long Action Camp at Kennedy Lake, starting with Forest Watch: the art of keeping a public eye on corporate logging practices. Hiking into the active areas, looking at cutblocks and watching the treatment of and effect on creeks and other bodies of water. Speaking for salmon. Reporting evidence of stream damage, unlawful cutting in biodiversity corridors, destruction of bear dens—that sort of thing. Extremely important work and another way of exercising our democratic rights other than by voting.

Another encampment set up on land near Victoria ran for four weeks. The Friends' "Rainforest Action Camp [RAC] August 1994" pamphlet talked about linking issues and oppressions, and creating safe spaces. "We hope to attract people who will respect the camp nonviolence code and the boundaries set up on such issues as drumming, smoking … sexism, racism, heterosexism, antisemitism, classism, ageism, speciesism, ableism, etc." Workshops and training took up the first half of the month. The second half consisted of daily actions in the city, enlightening Commonwealth Games visitors on the state of BC's forests: "Stolen-wealth Shames." Tzeporah had received a backroom offer: all her charges would be dropped if she could promise no protests during the Games. Putting aside the filthiness of the offer, how could the Crown believe one person held that much power over that many individuals? The Crown was not only utterly clueless, but had missed the point entirely of hundreds of arrests: this was a movement, not a dictatorship.

A Bear Watch meeting and dinner party was held over on čačatic. Someone had made a huge chocolate cake in three pieces: a bear's face and two paws, with almonds for claws. Sharon, the woman who had, on Naćaas, heckled Harcourt and suggested a logger change his career, ran around smearing icing on people's faces. I said no and ducked!

Somewhere in the Sound, Greenpeace locked themselves to a grapple yarder for a day. There were no arrests.

The next time I wrote a news release was for the action on July 26. The computer crashed, the story changed, I missed my deadline, a volunteer harangued me, I cried in the washroom. But the release got out, and better late than never. About eighty people from the lake camp demonstrated outside the Ministry of Forests in Port Alberni. Five were prepared to be arrested, including both Sushil and Betty. But the police backed down. They also refused to take Deputy Minister Chris Hayhurst, whom Betty placed under citizen's arrest for his part in breaking international law (clear-cut logging contravened three international treaties, including the UN Rio Earth Summit biodiversity convention). Our people kept Hayhurst out of the office all day.

Days later there was an action at the Port Albion Mac Blo office. There were four arrests, but Crown counsel phoned the Ucluelet police and told them not to lay any charges.

That night there was trouble at the Kennedy Lake camp: loggers making threats, yelling, pushing, even throwing rocks. A couple of days earlier, Bill and Paul had had their faces punched; this time Amy, Sushil, and I decided to visit the camp as support. We hadn't been involved on the ground, but we weren't willing to sit by while who-knows-what was happening.

The loggers were gone when we arrived. A few police stood around, and most of the camp was meeting around the fire. I'd heard that a friend of mine had been surrounded by angry loggers when she was alone at the junction at 5:30 a.m. I found her near the fire. We embraced, and she wept into my shoulder. We found ourselves standing in the centre of a huge circle of people holding hands and breathing deeply. People spoke of their fears, and of fear itself.

After work the next day I joined the demonstration at Interfor's office. Betty and Sergio were inside. They were soon arrested and held till the end of the working day. Again, not charged.

In mid-August, the RAC started its "Welcome to the Real BC" campaign, a banner hanging where Games-goers could not miss it. Iron Ron had been staying at the camp, seemingly with the intent of disorganizing it. On the fifteenth he was arrested for drumming.

On the twenty-second, our people occupied the Ministry of Environment to publicize the many violations of international treaties (environmental laws) signed by Canada. On the twenty-third and twenty-fourth, youths under eighteen occupied the Ministry of Forests. While there, they were refused water, food, and toilet use, all basic human rights. On the twenty-fifth, people locked themselves to doors in Ministry of Forests executive offices.

In September, I began putting out a little birdseed for the jays and juncos. One day I saw a red squirrel moving toward a banana slug on the outside windowsill. Indeed, it picked up the soft, sticky creature—I thought, with a shock, to eat—and proceeded to nibble birdseed off the slug's behind. The very same day, a bee was buzzing around my potted orchids when suddenly it was silenced by a jay, who ate it whole.

There were so many osprey sightings. These birds are magnificent, yet can be mistaken for a gull if only glanced from a distance. They dive from a height, emerge from the water, become airborne again, shake the water off themselves, and fly off, carrying a fish parallel to their bodies rather than parallel to their wings. At the cabin, I met a bat. I was on the deck when it flew close to my face, wings clicking, then hurled itself off through the air like a bird with an unreachable itch.

I found I could no longer take Sid down Browning Pass inlet trail. His neighbours felled trees right up to the boundary line (which also happened to be the first part of the trail), and over it. Our way was buried. Over time what was once forest became Abraham Drive and Tofino's Bible belt.

A full moon had just risen over Hiłthuuʔis one night when a single howl filled the air. Green and I hurried out onto the deck as more howls joined in. We sat listening as the moon's reflection shone on the ocean. The wolves had to have been across the inlet from us, on the shoreline beyond Ghost Isle.

High-pitched yowling ensued: a canine singalong. All too soon it abruptly stopped, and suddenly we were aware of the cacophonous beach below at low tide. It performed its own concert of squeaking, sucking, and squirting by clams, barnacles, and myriad other life forms.

Before we went in, an uncanny gurgling, perhaps from a mink or otter, came from down below, rather like something with a bubble in its throat. Then a heron startled us with its terrified squawking, as it flew in a panic from whatever had frightened it.

October 4, 1994, Japan had an earthquake that caused a tsunami to travel across the world at terrifying speed; it was due to hit Tofino at 4:05 p.m. Local beaches and waterfront homes were evacuated, boats moved. I was excited. I joined a crowd overlooking the harbour at four o'clock. The song "Blessed Be" filled my head as I imagined the water rising (not too high). I wanted Mama Earth to show us who was in charge. Someone reality-checked me by saying, "This is just nature. It's normal." Mere moments before 4:05 p.m., the warning was called off. The sea had come to the top of Long Beach, according to people who got into a plane and flew around.

But nobody in town saw anything except for the fire truck driving by. A joke was made of the "cancelled tsunami."

That month, the province charged MacMillan Bloedel under the federal Fisheries Act with "harmful alteration" of Winter Creek, a salmon stream in the Sound. For a while the case proceeded at a snail's pace. Then, in September '96, the case was dropped. Why? Because the provincial Crown prosecutor, Brian Rendell, ordered a stay of proceedings due to new "expert opinions" he had obtained which did not substantiate the charge. Why would Rendell choose to seek additional opinions, when he already had strong evidence against Mac Blo? He'd done it before, too. In Haida Gwaii, he sought additional opinions despite strong evidence against Fletcher Challenge and Crown Forest Industries, and the charges were stayed as a result. Rendell successfully prosecuted me and hundreds of other Clayoquot arrestees. As Maryjka put it: "If you're a corporate eco-vandal and lawbreaker, not to worry, but if you're a peaceful protester putting your conscience above the law, the justice (just-us) system will punish you."

While meetings continued, a marbled murrelet's nest was found and recorded in the Bulson, and songbird and bat studies were in place throughout the Sound.

We spent quite a bit of the autumn in Vancouver waiting for my nephew Rowan to be born; when we returned, a storm had tossed all three solar panels off the deck. They had hung there until our good neighbours Julie and Liz hauled them up. Rain had gotten inside the cabin and soaked half our bed. Our boat, at Jensen's dock in town, nearly sank. Kevin bailed it and rescued the battery.

One November afternoon Green was in town working at FOCS. I was in bed trying to nap when I heard such an uproar of canine voices that I leapt up, threw on my coat and boots, and crept out onto the deck to listen. They were not howling, but barking and squealing and yipping and yapping. The noise was so near I believed they must be around the comer, near our dock. I was straining my neck in that direction when I heard another sound, altogether different. It was coming from the water to my right (east). This puffing, blowing noise was louder, and somehow larger, than porpoises' short, sharp exhaling and drawing-in of breath. I whirled around. The canine noises suddenly ceased. Below me was a pod of orcas.

I stood with binoculars glued to my eyes, full-body-clenching with excitement. The whales were surfacing in all directions, feeding. A mother was towing her young one, while a male's long dorsal fin pointed up out of the water, tall, black, and proud, striking against the grey sea. Their breathing was a beautiful sound. It brought me back memories of being a child at the aquarium, but this time the animals were free: in their natural habitat, with lots of space, among family members.

After a moment I charged down the trail to the beach. But as I arrived the whales were moving away, toward Tofino, the same route we took our boat nearly every day. Orcas, proper name Kakawin, in the sea. It's so natural, but it was a surprise to me. I was never a good whale watcher on outside waters, where the swell makes me sick. I stood among the barnacles for a minute after they had gone and remembered the wolves—if that's what I had first heard. I thought of searching for them, but I would be heard or scented long before I could come near them. There was no more barking, squealing, or yipping. It remains a mystery, and there were always plenty of those. I was grateful to have been disturbed from my nap.

November 21, 1994, marked ten years since the Meares Island (Wanačis-Hiłthuuʔis) blockade. After two years of negotiations in the early '80s between FOCS, loggers' unions, Indigenous officials, and Mac Blo, the latter pulled out of the process and prepared to help themselves to the precious island that hosts the Big Trees Trail and Opitsat village. On this day in 1984, Tlaoquiahts and non-Indigenous locals joined together to stop a boat full of Mac Blo loggers from landing at C'is-a-qis bay. And kept it up through the winter. In celebration of this anniversary, people would be going out to C'is-a-qis to raise the Tribal Park sign once again (I couldn't join them). The previous night a potluck dinner had been held in the school gym, organized by FOCS. About 140 people attended. Photographer Adrian Dorst gave a slide show. I especially loved the slide of a cougar in a tree. Colonial law has still not judged who has the right to Wanačis-Hiłthuuʔis, but others have. And thanks to the original blockaders, Tofino (Načiks and Kwisaqs) still enjoys the rare view of nearly all old growth from its harbour.

Mike Mullin was emcee for the evening; he had been involved at C'is-a-qis. As children provided an amusing backdrop of chaos on the jungle gym, Mike described the impressiveness with which Tlaoquiaht Moses Martin greeted the loggers that day. "Welcome to our garden. There will be no logging here," Moses had said, and folded his arms with authority. How could anyone have argued with him? He was later charged with obstructing the colonial law, but the charge was dropped. Not until 2024, in *Tofino and Clayoquot Sound: A History*, did I learn of an RCMP officer confronting Nuučaańuł Tribal Councillor George Watts, who stood beside Moses forty years previously. The cop said, "I've got room to put a thousand Indians in my jail." George Watts replied, "You go ahead. We'll bring a thousand more."

I've told the story of Mike's wife Linda in another memoir, describing the thirtieth anniversary celebration of that blockade. In 1984, Linda—shaking with nerves—told Mac Blo point blank that their machines would have to run over her and her children to log that island. It was her way of defending the future for everyone's kids and grandkids.

At this 1994 anniversary celebration, Moses himself spoke briefly, restating that his commitment was still strong: "Those trees are still standing, and hopefully will for at least another hundred years."

Mary Martin spoke about feeling annoyed saying "Clayoquot" when she knew it was—and *she* was—Tlaoquiaht, and that she took time to learn to pronounce the original name. Her grandmother taught her to be positive and to send any negative thoughts out to the universe. "We are First Nations people; we are not a rock and roll 'band.' We are not Indians; we are not from India. We have to define ourselves. For too long, others have been defining what we are."

Joe David was the artist who carved the six-and-a-half-metre tall cedar man raised on the parliament lawn in Victoria ten years previously. Carved figures used to have one hand held out, but the other held back, in caution of the white folks. He had moved the arms of his cedar man so that both were held out. This signified that we were all working together to save the land now. The hands say: "Welcome to the struggle. Welcome to the family of Earth."

> I feel there is something ultimately compelling about local people struggling to maintain the beauty that surrounds them; something inviting about people who are working hard for no pecuniary gain and who are peaceful in their nature. The backdrop for our struggle looms large, making it all the more visible. We have huge multinational timber companies gobbling up enormous volumes of forest for raw log export and telephone books, and we have the physical backdrop of one of the largest remaining tracts of glorious ancient temperate rainforest on planet Earth.
>
> —Valerie Langer

RANKIN COVE, FAIRY CREEK, ET AL.

INTERFOR TRASHES CLAYOQUOT BIOSPHERE
ROADLESS RAINFOREST TOO RARE TO WRECK
THERE GOES THE FUTURE
NO MORE ROADS
ENOUGH ALREADY!
CLAYOQUOT: GETTING WORKED OVER (banner)

In the summer of '95, FOCS was present to witness road building in Shark Creek, Clayoquot Sound. At the mouth of the creek is a series of waterfalls. The lowest of the falls cascades into an ocean tidal pool which was said to be frequented by basking sharks. (Those sharks were extirpated from the Sound—after much abuse from DFO, even installing huge blades on ship bows—apparently with the introduction of salmon farms.) The day before blockading was to begin, Mac Blo withdrew from the valley due to negotiations with FOCS. This was a first. However, the company did not promise a permanent pullout.

> We have seen more changes in forestry in the last two years than we saw in the previous fifteen, but should we feel satisfied? Smaller clearcuts across the valleys and up the mountainsides, swaths of trees blowing down in the stream buffers and between cuts, landslides, streams plugged with logging debris, denuded steep slopes. The gamut of environmental atrocities still happen even here in Clayoquot Sound but it's happening with more

> paper work, some changes, and on a *slightly* smaller scale. The fact is you can take steps in the right direction but if they are too small or too slow you still miss the boat! One recent government cutting permit allowed clearcutting in an old-growth stand even though Interfor acknowledged wolf, bear and cougar populations were using the stand.
>
> —FOCS summer '95 newsletter

That July, the BC government accepted the approximately 120 recommendations of its "Scientific Panel for Sustainable Forest Practices in Clayoquot Sound." But the Science Panel had to adhere to the 1993 CLUD, which designated 74 percent of Clayoquot's forests as open to logging. Some of the new Science Panel permits (cutblocks logged while supposedly taking recommendations as "guidelines") were soon logged, and they were definitely clearcuts. Meanwhile, the companies were developing logging plans for the last pristine watersheds.

BAD ATTITUDE

Interfor - for building a crappy road up Rolling Stone Creek, not letting it settle and then driving machinery on it in torrential downpours, causing the road to melt into the creeks. For placing siltation barriers everywhere but on the road, and, last but not least, for clearcutting again in the newest Science Panel cutblock in Clayoquot Sound. You've really flubbed it this time (again). We hope the Attorney General fines you the full million dollars and three years in jail for breaking Section 45 of the Forest Practices Code.

MacBlo - for trying to pass off little patches of trees in the middle of a clearcut as a major shift of consciousness, for punching a new road up the very steep slopes in the lower Bulson, and for burning your slash piles in the creeks in cutblock 7B during salmon spawning season. We hope some agency will make you pay for your blatant disregard for the fish. Until then we are distributing the pictures of your arrogance far and wide.

Calling it in Friends of Clayoquot Sound newsletter.

On the morning of January 17, 1996, several new landslides on Wanačis and Catface Mountain could be seen from Tofino. Helicopters reported at least sixty new slides in the Sound over a few days of heavy rainfall. Yet these were not record rains. It was an average winter on the west coast.

Many slides occurred on slopes very recently logged; some were additions to existing slides on previously clear-cut mountainsides. Other slides mowed down established second growth. Video footage showed mud-filled, chocolate-coloured lakes. Many salmon streams would continue to be affected.

The fact that a few of the slides occurred in old growth informed us that the thin layer of soil on mountainsides is fragile to begin with. The second growth slides told us that replanting a slope after clearcutting it does not necessarily stabilize the soil, even when a plantation has reached several decades of age. That some of the slides came from new clearcuts begged the question: Why was logging on steep slopes allowed? And why was the Science Panel not putting a stop to these destructive practices?

I would add: How many animals were killed in the slides? How many in the food chain would suffer from resulting pollution of salmon streams?

> By the late 1950s, logging trucks had replaced steam locomotives, leaving many mountainsides on Vancouver Island zigzagged with steep gravel roads, as trucks retrieved timber ever higher on mountain slopes. These roads became so steep that some logging trucks carried 1,350-litre tanks of water to cool their brakes as they negotiated the switchbacks on their way down carrying log loads of over 100 tonnes.
>
> —Margaret Horsfield and Ian Kennedy

The Friends had expanded its mission statement since 1992. Now it read thus:

> To be peaceful and courageous advocates for the protection and defence of the ancient forest, fish and wildlife, air, land and water of Clayoquot Sound.

Statement of policies:

1. We recognize that Clayoquot Sound is a priceless natural heritage to be protected though legislation.
2. We recognize the Tla-o-qui-aht and Ahousaht declaration of Meares Island as a Tribal Park and support its legal adoption.
3. We support legislation requiring restoration of areas which have been devastated by clearcutting, road building or landslides caused by development in Clayoquot Sound (and British Columbia), to be paid for by the companies responsible for the damage.
4. Our responsibility is to oppose decisions which harm the integrity of ecosystems.
5. We call for legislation to abolish clearcutting.
6. We call for a halt to logging in primary forests and support ecoforestry in secondary forests.
7. We call for a halt to the export of all raw logs or industrially modified raw logs.
8. We promote reduced consumption of wood and wood fibre products and support tree-free alternatives.
9. We call for abolition of Tree Farm Licenses and corporate control of public forests.
10. We oppose mining in Clayoquot Sound due to the known environmental hazards of mineral extraction.
11. Due to hazards to wild fish stocks, pollution of waters and impacts on sea life, we oppose fish farming in Clayoquot Sound. We encourage restoration of wild salmon runs and protection of their natural habitat.
12. We strongly oppose sport and trophy hunting.

First Nations:

> The Friends of Clayoquot Sound recognize the historical injustices perpetrated by non-native cultures on First Nations peoples and cultures, and respect First Nations' right to self-governance and their struggles for justice.

On summer solstice, 1996, the Greenpeace ship *Moby Dick* came into Clayoquot Sound waters in the early hours of the morning. Several Friends of Clayoquot Sound were waiting to meet it. In daylight, Greenpeace inflatables motored to shore at a log sorting station in Rankin Cove used by both Mac Blo and Interfor. Greenpeace was known for its Zodiacs. It was heard later that one of the workers on shore shouted sarcastically amidst much laughter: "Hey, look—Zodiacs! It must be Greenpeace! Look sharp, everyone!"

I wish I'd seen his face when three people chained themselves to a log loader in the process of sorting logs to be shipped out of Clayoquot. One or two loggers attempted and failed to pull the activists off. All four access roads leading from the camp were also blocked.

By the time I heard about it, three FOCS directors were already chained: Maryjka, Betty, and Sergio. We couldn't communicate with the *Moby Dick* due to technical difficulties at the office. The ship had followed its Zodiacs and anchored at Rankin. While the media kept calling, I had nothing to tell them they didn't already know. It was a familiar source of frustration. Luckily it didn't last.

At one point I found myself frantically packing (having borrowed a friend's clothes) to spend the night at the action site. I got a ride in an oyster skiff all the way to the pretty green ship. Everyone on board was tired but friendly; the deckhands blew me away with their cheery confidence and ability. They were always busy doing something.

I looked toward shore and saw a huge building sticking out onto the water: luxury floating accommodation for Interfor and Mac Blo employees. A deckhand, Richele, buzzed me over to the dock.

I walked up a dirt road into a big clearcut full of log piles, trucks, and machinery. Green and various other people were sitting on a stray log. Hundreds of swallows were swooping and diving all around us, feasting on mosquitoes and no-see-ums. Unfortunately, this didn't stop the bugs from feasting on us, too.

The forest surrounding the area brought forth some interesting inhabitants, like a woodpecker and a modest black bear. I say modest, because it just ate and ate while we crowded nearby ooh-ing and ahh-ing. It never once lifted its head to look at us.

Nobody but nobody had bug repellent. I spent some time sitting on the loader with an old friend, who was chained to it. I rubbed orange peel on her face and neck, but it was futile.

No workers appeared, except a security guard and a company cook. We were prepared for anything, because one activist had seen a convoy of vehicles full of loggers heading our way. Bruce Hornidge wrote in his logging memoir: "I sat on a log about fifty metres from the demonstrators … I was dripping saliva from my teeth, I despised them so much."

The cook kept asking those locked to the loader, "You *sure* you don't want to surrender?" As soon as he found out we were vegetarians, he wanted to know if we were in the habit of eating chicken. And when the bear was doing its thing, he kept yakking to anyone near him, "I'll give you a dollar if you go and jump on his back! Ha ha!"

Why were we hanging around putting up with this, anyway? Well, for one thing, Interfor was still logging in Rolling Stone valley even after being fined for violating section 17(1) of the Forest Practices Code. The company had not properly maintained a road, so it eroded into salmon stream tributaries of Rolling Stone Creek.

Moreover, after over a hundred slides (or "rain events") on steep slopes, companies were continually permitted to log almost vertically. New term named by our side: not clearcuts but clear*cliffs*.

Furthermore, piles of "waste" logging debris/slash were being burned in the valleys called Bulson and Tranquil.

Yet another motive for "locking on" was the fact that three new cutblocks had been issued in the Bulson even though the Science Panel considered it to be pristine and recommended that logging in pristine areas be deferred pending the outcome of scientific assessments. It seemed that these studies were going to be underway during logging! Assess-and-log, talk-and-log. Plus, salmon stream restoration was supposed to have begun in the lower watershed before they were to log the upper watershed. Didn't happen. So for three days, good people shut down all logging operations in the Sound.

Shortly after dark a group of us lay on the ground trying to rest. I was fully clothed, in head-to-toe rain gear and hiking boots, in someone else's sleeping bag. (I had been told to leave all my gear on the ship in case we were required to make a quick evacuation.) The ground was hard, the air was cold and thick with flying, biting things—and then it started to rain. I tried to ignore it. After a while Green whispered, "Do you want to move to a tent?"

It was the only tent, and we shared it with Jacqueline Windh and her friend. The sleeping bags were soaked, so we used them as pillows. By this time, I was wet *inside* my rain gear. Soon the birds were singing to wake the dead. I heard a nighthawk among them. Then Betty's "hog-calling" voice and laughter filled the air as she took her shift on the loader. Her lock and chains rattled against the machine.

We got up and walked around to get warm. The bugs were worse, and we caught the next inflatable to the *Moby Dick.* On board, there was no bug repellent. People were working on a news release amidst a buzz of anticipation. The front page of the *Sun* said something inappropriate like "Indians want Greenpeace out of Clayoquot."

Tzeporah sat smoking. The day before, she had been in a news conference in Vancouver that was stormed by IWA members. Then she had met with twenty elected Chiefs from the Nuučaan̓uł Tribal Council in Port Alberni. They shouted angrily at her for hours. Finally, driving back to Tofino that night, a logger she recognized ran her off the road with his pickup. Her car flipped, but landed upright.

The details, in her book *This Crazy Time*, make a gripping read.

Greenpeace and FOCS hadn't followed protocol. We hadn't asked permission from the Chiefs to do the blockade. I believe that eco-groups have learned better since then. Greenpeace didn't even ask permission for the *Moby Dick* to enter Tlaoquiaht waters. And all night the word went out to every Indigenous community to come out and show Greenpeace whose territory it was in.

We all assembled on the main deck to be briefed on plans for the day. Then Tzep, Valerie, and Karen were whizzed away to meet the Chiefs at First Street dock in town. They kept in touch with us by radio. Every few minutes a different message arrived.

"They wouldn't talk. They're on their way."

"There's forty of them."

"They could be on board in thirty minutes."

"I doubt they'll arrive before an hour."

The video guy and photographer were to stay on board and be ready. I was supposed to watch the videographer's back. I left Green helping to sort life saving gear and went below to lie down for ten minutes in Richele's bunk. Soon the noise grew from above: feet were running around rather than walking. I dragged myself up and climbed on deck.

Everyone except the captain and a few deckhands had vanished. The deckhands were locking doors, tying ropes, strapping things down, "battening down the hatches," even pulling Zodiacs out of the water with a crane. I asked a deckhand what was going on. "We've done this a million times before," she said smiling, relaxed. "We just want to make sure we're not at a disadvantage if there are any surprises."

A couple of motorboats carrying a few loggers had approached and gone to shore. The blockaders were still chained, so everyone had gone over. I was stuck on board, on my own, useless.

I leaned on the railing, gazing over toward the shore, anxiety beating in my chest. Then suddenly I saw the whole thing as if from a distance: myself standing on board *Moby Dick*, my state of agitation, the lock-down situation, and the knowledge that at any minute, we could be swarmed by many potentially hostile people. I simply observed it all. I felt detached and no longer worried. I knew the self that stood leaning and straining for shore chose to be worked up, that it was a form of adrenaline. Slowly and comfortably the clarity of that moment gave way to a calm excitement, and I went to see if I could be of any help to the remaining crew.

Soon Val, Tzep, and Karen pulled up and got on board. They withdrew to the kitchen to prepare for the meeting. I didn't know how forty people were going to fit in there.

All was quiet on deck again. Until I heard, in the distance, a boat approaching. I stared until I could make it out. It was a big blue one, and it was moving fast. Too fast. It was the Opitsat water taxi, and it burned right on by, creating a wake that turned the *Moby Dick* into a see-saw.

Then another boat approached. It passed. Then another, and another. One of them was almost as big as *Moby Dick* itself—the *Spirit of Marktosis*, an Ahousat ferry. None of the passengers waved or looked. Suddenly I realized that Valerie and the others hadn't come out of the kitchen.

As soon as I set foot in the kitchen, I could see that they did not know. I could not get the words out fast enough. "They've gone—straight to shore—"

"They're gone—?"

"—to the dock?!"

The women rushed out and were in a Zodiac in seconds. I was not ready to go and I didn't want to slow them down. In truth, I didn't want to be stuck without rain gear either. Tzep yelled, "We'll try to bring them back here." As soon as they were gone more boats came. Some carried white men: people from Share BC. Just as I was thinking that there must be a lot more than forty Indigenous folks in attendance, a seaplane descended and I plugged my ears against the noise.

Eventually, the Chiefs boarded the ship. I helped hoist some of them on board. It was a gesture, really; most of them didn't want help. I said hi to one I knew. He looked up, startled. "Hello," he replied, grinning. Each one had their hand shaken by the captain with the greeting: "Welcome on board. I'm Bart—cap'n."

No loggers, Share members or cameramen came. On shore, the blockades still held. Green was one of the last to return.

"You left me!" I said.

"I thought you were sleeping! Didn't want to wake you!"

The Chiefs crammed into the kitchen. It was standing room only, and the air soon became stuffy. I was the last one in, squished against the wall by the door. Suddenly it went dark.

"Oops," I muttered, and flicked the light switch back on. Every time someone went out and was replaced by someone else coming in, that person would lean against the wall, put the light out, mutter "oops" and flick it on again as soon as humanly possible.

A man from Ucluelet spoke. "You say you've been to sixty countries," he said to Bart. "Well, I haven't been to many countries. You, you're from Ontario. I love a bit of rock a little south of here. And I'm not the kind of guy who can just up and move to Toronto and say 'God, I love this place!"

Someone muttered, "I don't think anyone's ever said that about Toronto."

Low laughter filled the humid room.

"The point is we've been here thousands of years and we're not planning on going anywhere. We ARE the environment!" That phrase rang out many times during the meeting. There were raised voices and some foul language. Twenty-five men pointing fingers at three women. To Tzeporah, it was mellow compared to the previous day's meeting in Port Alberni, during which she had succumbed to tears.

There were apologies for breach of protocol from the captain, from Greenpeace, and from FOCS. A bowl of peanuts was passed around and I watched Chief Francis Frank eat a cookie. Maybe this was our job as allies: to listen. However hard life might seem for me, it's been a lot harder for Indigenous nations. They have seen their land razed as if they were invisible, their children stolen and even killed.

It was people of European heritage who gave smallpox-infected blankets to the Chiefs' ancestors, Europeans who stole the land and set up the Canadian reservation system, Europeans who banned the potlatch. My forbears were from the so-called UK. People who looked like me tried to erase the culture, history, and identity of Indigenous nations in this country. I am not responsible for these historical atrocities. However, I am a participant in a colonialist oppressive society and have benefited from having white skin, whether or not I was conscious of that participation and those benefits.

One of the Chiefs said to the activists, "You can leave now with some dignity, and we will meet again in two weeks. Otherwise, I'm prepared to stay on this ship for as long as it takes."

All parties agreed to make a joint statement to government, logging companies, and media. Activists agreed to suspend blockades on the condition that negotiations would begin on issues such as intact valleys and the speed of implementation of Science Panel recommendations. Greenpeace and FOCS publicly acknowledged our breach of protocol for not discussing our activities with the Chiefs prior to the action. Nuučaańuł nations "committed to facilitate a meeting with all parties in two weeks to address the concerns of the protesters and work toward finding a solution to the issues that led to this conflict," said the news release.

"Then the Chiefs went to speak with the Interfor people in the logging camp," recalled Valerie in the 2023 celebratory group text. "After which we agreed to take down the blockade and Interfor agreed to engage in the discussions about not logging intact areas."

Soon after quitting the room, I got a ride to shore and let blockaders know what to expect. Naturally, there were some disappointed faces. Maryjka grumbled. Nor did Betty want to cave in. Then FOCS, Greenpeace, and the Chiefs arrived and walked en masse to each blockade. Tzeporah read the statement and asked activists to move aside. Before the cameras, Betty unlocked herself with a flourish. Francis Frank thanked everyone and shook hands. The atmosphere was friendly.

I was now more than ready to go home. An inflatable was prepared to take FOCS to Tofino. There were hugs and farewells all around, and the whole crew waved from the deck of the ship as we moved off. Suddenly, a small speedboat appeared. In it was the process server—the Weasel—who had been handing out injunctions forever! He had read the injunction through a megaphone every morning on every blockade in my memory. He was also known to open the front doors of people's homes and toss SLAPP suit notices inside.

His boat came closer and he beckoned knowingly with his finger.

"Step on it!" someone cried to our driver. "Accelerate!"

We all took up the chant, with much laughter. Our Zodiac burned out of there and the Weasel gave up the chase.

Half an hour later, a motley crew of tired activists lugged our gear up from the dock. There to greet us, looking very self-satisfied, was the Weasel. He handed Sergio, Betty, and Maryjka each a stack of extremely white papers. These weren't injunctions, but notifications/warnings of application for injunction.

"How did you get here before us?" we asked incredulously.

He answered by flapping his arms up and down.

I heard stories after that day. That as soon as our lock-down had begun, a Mac Blo helicopter landed on a Chief's front lawn. There was a whispered accusation in town that the Chiefs were acting as the logging companies' police force. The blockade could have threatened sensitive treaty negotiations with the provincial government. The Chiefs, naturally, would not want to lose all they had gained. They were finally procuring some control over what happened to their land; would they let a bunch of ecos ruin such achievements? Their people were poor. Yet those men insisted it was our breach of protocol that caused their anger. I had no trouble imagining Harcourt making a condition-laden offer to the Nuučaaňuł nations.

A day or two later I was answering phones at FOCS.

"Hello? Friends of Clayoquot Sound."

"Yeah, I just wanted to say that I think you guys really sold out by agreeing to cancel the blockade. Don't you know Francis Frank is an industry man? There's nothing he wants more than logging in Clayoquot. That's how he's going to employ his people."

"May I ask who's calling?"

"You don't have to be nice to those guys. They're elected Chiefs, not hereditary. That's our system, not theirs. They're corrupt. Been co-opted by companies and government long time ago. You know they get paid nine hundred bucks a day to sit at the treaty tables?"

"Hey, I'm Chris, and I'd like to know who you are," I said, starting to feel annoyed.

"Breach of protocol is a cover-up issue. Why are the Friends the bad guys for not acknowledging protocol? Look, sport fishermen, commercial fisheries, resorts, clam diggers, oyster farms: none of these guys acknowledge protocol. It's all Clayoquot land. The village of Tofino doesn't acknowledge protocol!"

I mouthed wordlessly to Green, beckoning him over.

"Did M and B follow protocol? Did Interfor? Not. I mean Paul Watson, much as I can't stand the guy, before Sea Shepherd entered these waters he radioed ahead and asked permission. The natives don't agree with his stuff, tree spiking, y'know, but they were impressed because he's one of the very few who ever bothered with protocol."

"Look, Mr.—have you read the joint statement? The blockades weren't cancelled, they were suspended. The economy has to diversify. All parties issued a warning to government and companies that change isn't happening fast enough."

"Yeah, I've read it. Yeah, right. Like you believe the Chiefs are neutral and caught between environmentalists and—"

"I didn't say what I believe."

"You know that one of them stopped a British company from cancelling a $25 million dollar contract with M and B. And he's mad, 'cause M and B didn't even thank him? I'll tell you what, friend. If you guys stand for no cutting, stand for no cutting. Keep it simple. I know it's scary when you're surrounded by big angry guys, closing in around you. Let me know when the next blockade happens."

"You'd have to identify yourself for me to do that."

He hung up. Neither Green nor I had recognized the voice. Twenty-eight years later Tzeporah's husband Chris Hatch, in his online *National Observer* column [Zero] Carbon, reminded readers, "We, non-Indigenous tree-huggers, made dreadful mistakes both in protocol and in practice. In retrospect, it's amazing some of them were not irreparable."

For one month in the summer of 1996, we promised not to blockade. Meanwhile, another cutblock went to the chainsaws. The first all-concerned-parties meeting was another browbeating of activists, demanding we shelve our campaigns and go along with the Science Panel's status quo. It was supposed to have been about pristine watersheds. The companies' first and foremost concern was, were we going to blockade? They were scared.

Indigenous nations banished FOCS, Greenpeace, and the Rainforest Action Network to a back room with the logging companies. After twelve gruelling hours of meetings, Mac Blo and Interfor agreed to an economic transition strategy based on the possibility that there may never be company access to intact watersheds in Clayoquot Sound! It was still in theory, but was good news. Also, the two corporations agreed to be willing to discuss delaying entry into intact valleys to make sure inventories would not be conducted under economic pressures from logging interests. Intact systems are such precious blueprints.

One week after the blockade was suspended, the *Haida Brave*, a giant log-loading and transporting barge, filled up at Rankin Cove and took its weighty cargo of trees out of the Sound, the province, and the country forever.

On July 18, I came face to face with a cougar. It moved like a golden phantom, and uttered a single wistful meow before departing. Around the same time, a juvenile hummingbird attempted to find nectar in Green's nostril.

In April of 1997, Mac Blo signed an agreement to form a joint venture corporation (JVC) with the Nuučaańuł to log in the northern portion of Clayoquot Sound. The Nuučaańuł owned 51 percent of the corporation and Mac Blo owned forty-nine percent. The JVC intended to log up to forty-thousand cubic metres of wood each year, probably starting in '98. The area most likely to be logged first was Flores Island. I felt shocked to think of Flores coming under the chainsaw.

MB also proposed a second JVC to log in the southern portion of the Sound. Between the joint ventures, added to Interfor's cut, so much timber would be up for grabs that the companies would have to move into the remaining unlogged valleys to get it all.

> The intention of the JVC is to provide a profit base for a larger Native economic development corporation called 'Mamook Corporation'. First Nations have to build a capital base to invest in other economic development activities. Eventually, they hope to bring down unemployment and poverty levels in their villages. We have great hopes that Mamook and the JVC see options for development without touching the last remaining intact watersheds.
>
> —FOCS

Bedwell River valley: a private lot, definitely a clearcliff, was logged right to the banks of a small stream. A landslide and logging slash quickly swept down the stream. This example was not permissible under the Forest Practices Code, but the code did not apply to private land.

At a science conference in which scientists stood up to introduce themselves by describing their impressive specialties, Valerie rose and declared: "Hi, I'm Valerie Langer and I make outrageous statements with no scientific backup and then I wait for science to catch up." The Science Panel was finally repeating what defenders had been saying about Clayoquot Sound for seventeen years. Why do we allow taxpayers' money to be spent getting scientists to prove clearcutting is damaging to ecosystems? If they were trying to prove it was not damaging, they would have given up long ago and saved us a lot of money.

Val visited Tofino's Interfor office (when it had one) to view cutting plans. She had difficulty getting any work done because so many Interfor staff wanted to speak with her. Then the secretary was giggling and saying, "Valerie, telephone."

On the line was Matt, FOCS campaigner. "The green monkey has swallowed the blue fish," he told her.

"What are you talking about?"

From the *Vancouver Sun*, January 8, 1997: "MacMillan Bloedel is shutting down its logging operations in Clayoquot Sound for the entire year, saying costs, delays and uncertainties make logging impossible. ... [The company is] offering severance packages and buyouts as a way of ending uncertainty for workers." Sorting and other small-scale operations continued. Mac Blo expected "a drastically reduced operation (could) start up again" in 1998. Not exactly a Just Transition. Ultimately, MB was bought out by Weyerhaeuser for $2.45 billion.

Interfor, meanwhile, continued to apply for cutting permits, and appealed its conviction for bad logging, since under the Science Panel convictions added up against you. FOCS applied for and were granted Intervener Status and gave evidence against Interfor during the appeal trial. Interfor subsequently lost the appeal.

The company planned to log in Virge Creek valley and on Catface Mountain Range, and was now cutting in Rolling Stone valley in two Science Panel-approved cutblocks. It also wanted to log the Sydney, where we had learned how to survey for marbled murrelets with Stephanie Hughes, Cosmo, and a bear. The time had come for forest defenders to meet with huge businesses like Scott Paper and convince them to boycott logging giants. Which they did—and they did. More and more corporations agreed to cancel their contracts, including the *New York Times*.

The next premier, Glen Clark, embarked on his own personal smear campaign against Greenpeace. One thing was clear, he was wrong when he claimed environmentalists didn't know what was going on in the forests. Forest Watch was a vital program that trained caring citizens across the province.

By 1997, Fletcher Challenge, under the name of TimberWest, had plans to put a bridge across the Kaxi:ks waterfall, and clear-cut that area. Citizens prevented it. It was citizens' actions which led to the creation of Carmanah Walbran Park. Special reunions take place there for anniversaries every decade. But there is citizen/activist presence there much more often than that.

Volunteers have built and maintained trails to help more people directly experience true ancient temperate rainforest. Friends of Carmanah Walbran, my old friend Pete included, have continued organizing "bio-blitzes" with biologists, mycologists, and naturalists in Kaxi:ks. These specialists have helped to prove that old growth is critical habitat for countless species, including those threatened or endangered. This remains a regular event, because in "Tree Farm Licence" (TFL) 46 Teal-Jones continues to hurt the central Walbran while Western Forest Products acts similarly against the upper Walbran in Tree Farm Licence 44. All unceded Pacheedaht territory. The spectacular Castle Grove is under threat, with its notable red cedar giants dubbed Karst Giant, Tolkien Giant, Castle Giant, Emerald Giant and Leaning Tower. "Over ninety percent of this province was taken without even the veneer of legality conferred by treaties elsewhere in Canada," wrote Arno Kopecky in the *Tyee*.

This has been a memoir of blockade times, so I cannot end without mentioning Fairy Creek/Ada'itsx, which peaked during the summer of 2021, despite the pandemic. The Rainforest Flying Squad organized actions across Canada. Indigenous people and non-Indigenous united to blockade clearcutting. Once again a precious place was (and still is) in danger of joining the ever-growing sea of clearcuts, thanks to Teal-Jones company. According to *Canopy of Titans*, some activists were arrested at both Tlaoquiat and Fairy Creek, including a ninety-two-year-old woman. I did not participate on-site, but sent money, signed petitions, and wrote letters and emails. Green found a second-hand EV so that he could take part in person. The blockades were far south of where we live.

Some methods were similar to previous times, like utilizing what was at hand, labouring day and night to cover the road with clearcut deadfall to impede vehicles. There were "flying dragons": a log installed across road or bridge, jutting out over the edge of a steep drop. A protector would sit hanging from the precarious end of that log, either in a hammock or on a platform, at risk of being knocked off and falling to their death. According to *Earth First! Direct Action Manual*, flying dragons' original name was simply a cantilever, used in both the Carmanah and the Walbran in 1993. Valerie's arrest at Sulphur Passage in 1988 was only slightly different in that she sat directly on the log itself. Rather more uncomfortable for hours at a time. But Fairy Creek heated up during a new time, with new advantages. A seventeen-year-old American, Joshua Wright, had been tracking old-growth logging via satellite imagery from Washington State.

> I saw that the Teal Jones Group was road-building into the headwaters of Fairy Creek. I was desperate to do something because I'd seen that pattern

> before. … After connecting with the Canadian activists, the blockade was started on August 9, 2020 and most of the time I was the only person who could reliably be connected to the Internet so, while there were Forest Defenders out at the blockades, I was the hub for coordinating between people and figuring out social media and trying to get the word out, trying to contact media, making press releases when stuff was happening on the ground and tracking whether logging approvals were going through. I was generally the person you could contact if you were out in the woods and you absolutely needed something to happen because I was going to be in service and up at any hour of the day trying to make it happen.
>
> —Joshua Wright

Satellite tracking and social media were a huge help to spreading the word and knowing where logging was. It gave activists a head start we often didn't have in the '90s. Fairy Creek ultimately replaced Clayoquot '93 as the largest act of civil disobedience in Canada with some 1,188 arrests, in often gruelling conditions in all seasons and weathers. Participants built huge and creative works of natural art as blockading structures: an elk, a Trojan horse, a giant bridge-spanning screech owl. Those who were able often bushwhacked for hours, carrying cement, tools, and chainsaws on their backs, dodging patrols. During daylight, supporters, media, and locked-down blockaders were separated from each other, corralled by the cops using yellow crime-scene tape. Tree-sitters were extracted via helicopter! And if we thought police violence was bad up in Tlaoquiat, it was shocking in Ada'itsx, with facial and genital pepper-spraying, broken bones, tents and cars destroyed, alleged exposure and cavity searches on-site.

PAUSE THE SAWS
NO ROADS INTO FAIRY CREEK
RESPECT EXISTENCE OR EXPECT RESISTANCE
ANCIENT FORESTS 4 CLIMATE JUSTICE
LET THE OLD GROWTH OUTGROW US
STOP TEAL JONES
ELDERS FOR ANCIENT TREES
DEFENDING UNCEDED ANCESTRAL FORESTS
GREED CUTTING THE LAST OLD GROWTH
B.C. NO POLICE STATE
WHO POLICES THE POLICE?
WHO'S POLICING THE RCMP?
MATRIARCHS SAY: HANDS OFF ANCIENT WOODS
A TREELESS FUTURE???
WORTH MORE STANDING

My publisher chose the title *Worth More Standing: Poets and Activists Pay Homage to Trees* for an anthology I edited. *Worth More Growing* became the youth volume. I was touched by her choices. As I type this present paragraph, there is a fundraiser in process for the publishing of Pacheedaht Elder Bill Jones and Karen Moe's book, *Flying the Coop: Fairy Creek and the Legacy of Pacheedaht Elder Bill Jones*. Elder Bill said, "During the Fairy Creek Blockades, I was able to finally totally realize myself and my self-worth." Karen has written that she "witnessed people who have the courage to love the future beyond themselves." And "we descendants of colonizers need to join the front lines that our culture has made necessary." There are also fundraisers for the trials and SLAPP suits that continue against citizen defenders.

The title of the book in your hands is meant as a verb. Blockade. As we go to press, the deferral on clearcutting the Fairy Creek watershed is about to end. Premier David Eby could permanently block the destruction of this watershed by declaring it saved and protected in a land-back contract with Elder Bill's people. Please check in with him at premier@gov.bc.ca.

Elder Bill Jones and the Screech Owl bridge barricade, Fairy Creek, 2021. Photo: Sodapop Liptrott

EPILOGUE

After five years on Stockham Island that property was sold and we were evicted. I began to live half the year in Tofino, the other half up the inlet in a floating cabin, surrounded by the ancient ancestral gardens of Wanačis-Hiłthuuʔis. Decades later I recognize more and more how rare and incredible this place is. Some find it scruffy, with many bare crowns sticking up among the green ones, but that is how you recognize old-growth forest. It is full of trees of all ages. So-called Meares is a lopsided horseshoe of watersheds and mountains, 8,500 hectares surrounded by a world of clearcuts and industry as usual. How is this reprieve possible? Because Mac Blo was originally given government permission to log 90 percent of it, lighting a fire inside local people? Because the Indigenous fought the colonial court? Because of people like Chief Nukmiis, Moses Martin, Maureen Fraser, Darlene Choquette, and Gloria Frank? Because of the tree spiking? Because the island houses Tofino's reservoir? Because whites and Aboriginals united in strength? With none of those efforts, this relatively small island would have been clear-cut just like everywhere else. Its marbled murrelets, bears, cougars, and qʷayaćiik (wolves) would have lost their homes. The water, air, and climate would all be degraded despite gradual greening-up with second growth. Mac Blo and Interfor would have been responsible for more desecration of culture and nature. As they have been—elsewhere in the Sound. As for the 2000 UNESCO Biosphere Reserve designation, it recognizes biodiversity, offers education and community grants, but cannot protect or defend against industry or development. For years I worked in Tofino art galleries, often checking with visitors and customers. Did they happen to know the sacrifices and struggles behind the incredible view outside that door? Locals grumble about the busy summers and the shrinking shoulder seasons, myself included. We had to choose. Clearcutting, or tourism. Meanwhile we have all benefited from the tourist economy, and it is time to give back via the Tribal Park Allies program.

In March 2024, people I knew were moving their floathome to flee the helicopter logging. Heli-logging can be seen as a way of preventing more roads, but it is both polluting and unsustainable. Any cutting of old growth is insanity at this point. If someone calls me "extreme" for demanding an end to old-growth logging, I remember that it's extreme to want to divide up the last sliver of pie rather than leave it so that we can breathe. It's extreme to continue cutting ancient rainforest, and radically daft to make the planet sick and destroy our grandchildren's future for a CEO's salary.

I've watched the town of Tofino lose its own mature trees, more every year, to developments. Our little group, Tofino Natural Heritage, writes letters. We have waited decades for a community tree protection bylaw. It's disappointing that people (including many arborists) continue to see old or dead trees as automatic hazards, so we try to dispel that myth and point out the vital importance of such trees. Replacing ancient carbon-sequestering wildlife habitat with a tiny potted plant that could easily die during new (and necessary) water restrictions is wasteful to say the least.

Back in the mid-'90s, Forest Watch exposed a cutblock approval that advised MB, if its workers were to find a bear den, to just fall the tree from higher up its trunk. If someone found a marbled murrelet nest in a tree, that stand wouldn't necessarily be left alone; the nest tree would likely be left standing in a clearcut from hell—until inevitable blowdown effect. And in the 2020s? It remains more of a right to turn a profit than to protect wildlife or our life support system. We know where we're headed now thanks to that warped reality.

Observing climate changes, every summer I white-knuckle through fire season—even in a rainforest. Complacency is not an option. An Indigenous activist said the term *protester* is an insult: "We are fighting to be who we are."

In response to the July 18, 2024, announcement of the newly protected 760 square kilometres, Gisele Martin responded,

> After GENERATIONS of work from many Nuučaanuł / Nuu-chah-nulth families and individuals, some illicit colonial land designations are being reformed to better respect our Indigenous land visions and Tla-o-qui-aht Tribal Parks declarations.
>
> British Columbia is now beginning to help us to protect the forest from BC! There was and is contact (it is still "early contact" now in terms of thousands of years of history), then attempted assimilation (tiičswiina mit niš!), then litigation (the supreme court of Canada could NOT prove canadian claim of ƛaʔuukʷiʔatḥ / Tla-o-qui-aht lands like Meares Island), then treaty negotiations (Canada did not negotiate in good faith), and now "reconciliation"! Hold your governments accountable, the work is ongoing!
>
> Happy for ʕaaḥuusʔatḥ and ƛaʔuukʷiʔatḥ Nations!
>
> ƛeekoo ƛeekoo to all our grandparents and leadership who worked towards upholding our existence.

In 2017, a special RCMP unit was formed to promote industry's interest, which seems both heinous and redundant. This Critical Response Unit has access to millions of dollars. It was the force mustered at Fairy Creek. According to *Women of the West Coast, Then and Now*, in 1988 on the Sulphur Passage blockade, ʔaahuusʔatḥ territory, the police said "No one stops the logging industry in British Columbia" as they arrested forest defenders. I've met good people who are cops. There is one who quit that squad to expose prevalent behaviours, attitudes, and practices. I never did pursue my own post-arrest grievance to the Complaints Commission. I'm glad my Gram didn't live to see the Fairy Creek brutality, or to feel the heat dome, or to see the tree deaths in Stanley Park, Vancouver, over the bridge from her home.

"Here comes the cliff," wrote Arno Kopecky. "We can slow down and shift course of our own free will, or we can plummet into the abyss and see how it feels when the machine finally arrives for us." There's a meme, a cartoon of an individual sitting with the planet against their back on ground that's tilted downhill. A cliff edge is near. This lone human is all that's keeping Earth from rolling off the brink. And there's a cop on either side of the person, trying to make the arrest.

Fairy Creek kids stop old-growth logging, 2021. Photo: Marnie Recker

TOP OLD GROWTH LOGGING

ACKNOWLEDGEMENTS

ʔuuščakšiƛ̓ʔick! Kleco, kleco! to the Indigenous nations whose ancestral gardens these lands are: Diitiidʔaatx̣ (Ditidaht), Pacheedaht, Qwabadiwa, ƛ̓aʔuukwiiʔatḥ (Tlaoquiaht), hiškwiiʔatḥ (Hesquiaht), and ʔaahuusʔatḥ (Ahousaht) peoples.

Also thank you to:

Readers of this book. Hišukiš čawaak; łaakšiƛ̓ allow me to ƛ̓eekooʔicuušʔaał naʔataḥ siy̓a huuḥtakšiiḥ.

I couldn't and wouldn't have dived in without Maureen Fraser, Joy Kogawa, Gordon Kogawa, Ann-Marie Metten, John Trinh, Peter Cressey, Max Goodwin, Sol Arbess, Valerie Langer, Maryjka Mychajlowycz, Kate Craig, Marlene Cummings, Sherry Marr, Fiona McCallum, Michael Mullin, Tzeporah Berman, Sergio Paone, Jill Thompson, Norleen Lillico, Garth Lenz, Warren Rudd, Adrienne Mason, Aaron Chapman, John Armstrong, Margaret Horsfield, Ian Kennedy, Beth Wilks, Chris Jang, Catherine Owen, Tina Norvell, Eileen Floody, Ruby Berry, Alison Fox, Jan Bate, Fireweed, Nicole Clifford Moen, Karen Moe, Friends of Clayoquot Sound as was, Joanna Streetly, Janice Lore, Eileen Park Robertson, Derek and Kathleen Shaw, Green Donaldsen, Gisele Martin, Tsimka Martin, Levi Martin, the Vancouver Island Regional Library, Dana Lyons, Bob Bossin, Starhawk, early arrestees (we see you!), Surfrider, Lilly Woodbury, Hannah Virtue, Marcie Callewaert, all the patient peeps who answered my questions or let me borrow their copies of various texts, and the rest of the credited songwriters. It was incredible to hear recorded, full versions of songs we sang on the blockades more than thirty years later. Thanks to Shirley and Keith Martin for lending me *Loggerheads* despite wondering if it might burst into flames at the touch of my hands. Continued thanks to the ever-gracious Rosanna Lapeyrouse at Mermaid Tales Bookshop. Salal bushels of gratitude to Brooke Wood and the Clayoquot Biosphere Trust for that neighbourhood grant! To the memory of those forest devotees resting in peace: Shirley Langer, Julie Draper, Gael Duchene, Jeff Beylard, Vera Webb, Dutch, and Carmen Castro. The awesome Ruth Masters. To everyone at Caitlin Press for always using Ancient Forest Friendly responsibly sourced paper. To my publisher Vici for adding baby goats to her menagerie of dogs and horses. To Sarah Corsie and Malaika Aleba for having my back and to Christina Myers and Meg Yamamoto for their editing excellence. To all three for encouragement and enthusiasm. We lost good people during the production of this volume. Rest in trees. Love, inspiration, laughter, adventure, remembrance, and above all action … for Shirley and Joe Langer, their grandson, Oscar, and Sherry's grandson, Josh.

SOURCES / BIBLIOGRAPHY

Online and Print Archives

friendsofcarmanahwalbran.com
Friends of Clayoquot Sound archived newsletters to 1990
focs.ca (online newsletter archives)
hakaimagazine.com
tribalparks.com/tribal-park-allies

Books and Essays

ʔiisaak in the garden by writers hired for Hotel Zed, Tofino. Hotel Zed, 2020.

Awesome Wildlife Defenders by Martha Attema. Ronsdale Press, 2021.

"B.C.'s 'War in the Woods' Grounds to Be Permanently Protected" by the Canadian Press, June 18, 2024, www.cbc.ca/news/canada/british-columbia/bcs-war-in-the-woods-grounds-to-be-permanently-protected-1.7239102.

Canopy of Titans: The Life and Times of the Great North American Temperate Rainforest by Paul Koberstein and Jessica Applegate. OR Books, 2023.

Cascadia Field Guide: Art, Ecology, Poetry edited by Elizabeth Bradfield, CMarie Fuhrman, and Derek Sheffield. Mountaineers Books, 2023.

Civil Disobedience by Henry David Thoreau. 1849 under a different title.

Clayoquot Mass Trials: Defending the Rainforest edited by Ron MacIsaac and Anne Champagne. New Society Publishers, 1995.

Clayoquot Perpetual Diary edited by Linda Rogers and Jill Thomas. Clayoquot Resource Centre/Manning Press, 1994.

Clayoquot: The Sound of My Heart by Betty Krawczyk. Orca Book Publishers, 1996.

"Commercial Whaling Ends" by Ben Mussett. British Columbia: An Untold History, bcanuntoldhistory.knowledge.ca/1960/commercial-whaling-ends.

Despair and Personal Power in the Nuclear Age by Joanna Macy. New Society, 1983.

Earth First! Direct Action Manual, 3rd edition. Earth First!, 2015.

Ecodefense: A Field Guide to Monkeywrenching, 2nd edition, edited by Dave Foreman and Bill Haywood. Ned Ludd Books, 1987.

Elements of Indigenous Style by Gregory Younging. Brush Education, 2018.

Empire of Wood: The MacMillan Bloedel Story by Donald MacKay. University of Washington, 1983.

Every Leaf a Hallelujah by Ben Okri. Apollo, 2021.

"Fairy Creek: Three Days in the Theatre of an Old-Growth Blockade" by Arno Kopecky, in *Points of Interest: In Search of the Places, People, and Stories of BC*, A Tyee Anthology, edited by David Beers and andrea bennett. Greystone Books, 2024.

"Heat: Giving Voice to a Silent Killer" by Chris Hatch. [Zero] Carbon with Chris Hatch, www.nationalobserver.com/newsletters/zero-carbon/2024/06/21/heat-giving-voice-silent-killer.

"It Happened Suddenly (Over a Long Period of Time): A Clayoquot History" by Valerie Langer, in *Witness to Wilderness: the Clayoquot Sound Anthology*, edited by Howard Breen-Needham, Sandy Frances Duncan, Deborah Ferens, Phyllis Reeve, and Susan Yates. Arsenal Pulp Press, 1994.

Itsuka by Joy Kogawa. Viking, 1992.

Loggerheads: A Memoir by Bruce Hornidge. Endless Sky, 2023.

Lone Cone by Dorothy Abraham. Self-published, 1961.

Meares Island: Protecting a Natural Paradise by Moses Martin et al. FOCS and WCWC, 1985.

"Petra Kelly's Legacy" by Andreas Jünger and Stephen Milder, Environment & Society Portal, www.environmentandsociety.org/

exhibitions/petra-kelly/6-petra-kellys-legacy.

Rare Bird: Pursuing the Mystery of the Marbled Murrelet by Maria Mudd Ruth. Rodale, 2005.

Settler: Identity and Colonialism in 21st Century Canada by Emma Battell Lowman and Adam J. Barker. Fernwood, 2015.

Spirits Rising: The Story of the Clayoquot Peace Camp, 1993 by Jean McLaren. Pacific Edge, 1994.

"Split Culture" by Susan Griffin, in *The Schumacher Lectures*, vol. 2, edited by Satish Kumar. Blond & Briggs, 1984. Via www.briangwilliams.us/natural-environment/susan-griffin.html.

"The Doing Is the Hope: The Forest Defenders of Fairy Creek" by Karen Moe. *Vigilance Magazine*, www.vigilancemagazine.com/post/the-doing-is-the-hope-the-forest-defenders-of-fairy-creek.

The Fifth Sacred Thing by Starhawk. Bantam, 1993.

The Great Transition by Nick Fuller Googins. Atria, 2023.

The Legacy of Luna by Julia Butterfly Hill. HarperOne, 2000.

The Lost Rainforests of Britain by Guy Shrubsole. William Collins, 2023.

The Man Who Climbs Trees by James Aldred. Mariner, 2018.

The Voyage of the Dawn Treader by C.S. Lewis. Geoffrey Bles, 1952.

"They're Cooking Faster! The Perseverance, Ingenuity and Art of the Fairy Creek Blockades" by Karen Moe. *Vigilance Magazine*, www.vigilancemagazine.com/post/they-re-cooking-faster-the-perseverance-ingenuity-and-art-of-the-fairy-creek-blockades.

Thinking Like a Mountain: Towards a Council of All Beings by John Seed, Joanna Macy, Pat Fleming, and Arne Naess. New Society Publishers, 1988. New Catalyst, 2007.

This Crazy Time: Living Our Environmental Challenge by Tzeporah Berman with Mark Leiren-Young. Knopf, 2011.

Tofino and Clayoquot Sound: A History by Margaret Horsfield and Ian Kennedy. Harbour Publishing, 2014.

Tree of Dreams by Laura Resau. Scholastic, 2019.

Wildlife & Trees in British Columbia by Mike Fenger, Todd Manning, John Cooper, Stewart Guy, and Peter Bradford. Lone Pine, 2006.

Women of the West Coast, Then and Now by Marnie Andersen. Sand Dollar Press, 1993.

Worth More Growing: Young Poets and Activists Pay Homage to Trees edited by Christine Lowther. Caitlin Press, 2022.

*Worth More Standing: Poets and Activists Pay Homage to Tree*s edited by Christine Lowther. Caitlin Press, 2022.

Film

Bones of the Forest directed by Heather Frise and Velcrow Ripper. 1995.

Forests Across Generations. Friends of Clayoquot Sound, 2020.

Fury for the Sound: The Women of Clayoquot directed by Shelley Wine. Telltale Productions, 1997.

Midnight Oil: The Hardest Line directed by Paul Clarke. 2024.

Rematriation directed by Alexi Liotti. 2022.

"Sulphur Passage (no pasaran)" directed by Nettie Wild. 1989.

The Road Stops Here directed by Velcrow Ripper. 1992.

War for the Woods directed by Sean Stiller and Geoff Morrison. 2022.

Song

"There's a fire on the mountain" lyrics adapted from Bob Bossin's "Fire on the Island."

"We Are the Power" copyright 2016 by Starhawk, recorded by Reclaiming; used with permission from Recording Quarterly.

"We are the flow" chant credited to Shekhinah Mountainwater.

"We All Come from the Goddess" by Z. Budapest, quoted with permission, zbudapest.com.

Groups

Ancient Forest Alliance

Canopy

Clayoquot Action

Environmental Youth Alliance

Friends of Carmanah-Walbran

Friends of Clayoquot Sound

Greenpeace

Rainforest Action Network

Rainforest Flying Squad

Sierra Club

Stand.earth (formerly ForestEthics)

Temperate Rainforest Action Coalition

Tla-o-qui-aht Tribal Parks

Wilderness Committee

GLOSSARY

bender: Shelter in the bush using curved branches and tarps.

cantilever: An anchor-dependent pole (log) extended across a portion of road or bridge to suspend a protector over a steep drop. Also called Flying Dragon.

crummy: A converted truck used to transport loggers to and from work.

CCF: Co-operative Commonwealth Federation was founded in 1933 as Canada's first political party representing workers and small farmers. Precursor to NDP.

NDP: New Democratic Party.

cork boots: The hefty footwear with cleats that loggers work in so that they have a grip when walking across slippery logs.

Forest Watch: Name used to describe the activities of trained citizens who monitored logging practices, looking in proposed cutblocks for discrepancies between the company's plans and what was actually on the ground; also looking at active and recently finished cutblocks and roads to assess compliance with various regulations (vague and weak as they were). Due to some findings, the Ministry of Forests ended up deferring final cutting approvals due to concerns raised by FW.

Raging Grannies: Groups of grandmother-aged women usually wearing hats festooned with flowers, inventing and performing protest songs set to the tunes of old standards.

Science Panel: Harcourt government-established Scientific Panel for Sustainable Forest Practices in Clayoquot Sound.

Share BC: Timber industry-oriented and -sponsored groups in Canada. Loggers pitted against us.

SLAPP suits: Strategic Lawsuits Against Public Participation that attack citizens for exercising our democratic rights. Powerful, wealthy corporations seek civil damages for criticism expressed in a public forum. Goal: intimidate us into silence.

tripod: A stable three-legged structure suspending a single person to block a road.

ABOUT THE AUTHOR

Christine Lowther resides in ƛaʔuukwiiʔath ha'huulthii in Nuučaan̓uł territory on Vancouver Island's west coast. She is the editor of *Worth More Standing: Poets and Activists Pay Homage to Trees* and its youth companion volume, *Worth More Growing*. She is the author of four poetry collections, most recently *Hazard, Home*. In 2014 the Pacific Rim Arts Society presented Christine with their inaugural Rainy Coast Award for Significant Accomplishment. Her memoir *Born Out of This* was shortlisted for the 2015 Roderick Haig-Brown Regional Prize. She won the Federation of British Columbia Writers' 2015 Nonfiction Prize and was shortlisted for the 2023 CBC Nonfiction Prize. Christine served as Tofino's Poet Laureate from 2020 to 2021.